NotDead YET

...and One or Two Other Good Things About Retirement

PATRICK FANNING

New Harbinger Publications, Inc.

Publisher's Note

This publication is designed to provide accurate and authoritative information in regard to the subject matter covered. It is sold with the understanding that the publisher is not engaged in rendering psychological, financial, legal, or other professional services. If expert assistance or counseling is needed, the services of a competent professional should be sought.

Distributed in Canada by Raincoast Books

Copyright © 2008 by Patrick Fanning
New Harbinger Publications, Inc.
5674 Shattuck Avenue
Oakland, CA 94609
www.newharbinger.com

All Rights Reserved
Printed in the United States of America

Acquired by Jess O'Brien; Cover design by Amy Shoup;
Edited by Carole Honeychurch

Library of Congress Cataloging-in-Publication Data
Fanning, Patrick.
  Not dead yet : --and one or two other good things about retirement / Patrick Fanning.
     p. cm.
  ISBN-13: 978-1-57224-552-5 (pbk. : alk. paper)
  ISBN-10: 1-57224-552-2 (pbk. : alk. paper)   1.   Retirement--Humor.   I. Title.
  PN6231.R44F36 2008
  306.3'80207--dc22

                                             2008039789

10 09 08
10 9 8 7 6 5 4 3 2 1   First printing

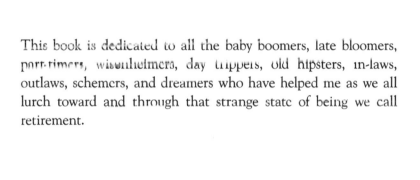

This book is dedicated to all the baby boomers, late bloomers, part-timers, wisenheimers, day trippers, old hipsters, in-laws, outlaws, schemers, and dreamers who have helped me as we all lurch toward and through that strange state of being we call retirement.

Contents

Part 1
Deciding to Retire

Part 2
Filling the Empty Hours

Part 3
Lifelong Learning

Part 4
Families

Part 5
Your Body

Part 6
Spirituality

PART 1

Deciding to Retire

1. Chapter One

This is really the Introduction, but nobody reads those, so I call it chapter one.

This is where writers traditionally try to convince you to read their masterpiece by telling you why they are qualified to write it, how much hard work it was, which important people helped them, and so on. I'm not going to bother because this book is obviously too short to be anybody's masterpiece.

Besides, if you're reading chapter 1, you've probably already paid for the book, so I'll be getting my 6.3 cents in royalties by and by whether you read it or not. Or perhaps you received this book as a gift, in which case we're both already ahead of the game.

That said, I think this may be the best book I've ever written. Certainly it was the most fun. But it won't be the best book you ever read because it's nonfiction. The best books are made-up true stories like Huck Finn or *The Lord of the Rings* trilogy.

Not Dead Yet, as you might guess from the title, is an irreverent look at retirement. I tried to write a reverent book first, but it was just too boring. I decided the book had to be funny or I would never get to the end of the damn thing.

But enough about me. Let's talk about you and retirement. Retirement is like a cliff that you approach very slowly, dither on the edge of, then jump off. After an exhilarating moment of free fall, you hit bottom and enter a long period of recuperation. Many people climb back up the cliff to re-enter the workforce for a while until they decide to jump off again. Wherever you are in this cycle, this is the book for you. It's written by me, the most qualified retirement expert in the galaxy, who has slaved away on it for twenty years with the help of sixteen Nobel Laureates.

No, just kidding. This is a toilet book—the kind with short chapters that you leave in the bathroom and pick up when you're in there on other business. The material is meant to make you smile, improve your digestion, and present a few practical, commonsense suggestions about retirement that you probably could have figured out for yourself.

In writing this book, I've discovered that there is a fine line between funny and stupid, so please skip over the stupid parts. There is also a fine line between funny and mean, which if I have crossed anywhere, oops, sorry. Not to mention the other fine lines between funny and weird, funny and silly, funny and lame, and so on. Funny is actually a tiny island in an ocean of fine lines. Welcome to my island, and I apologize if you get your feet wet.

2. AARP Is Stalking Me

When I turned fifty-five in 2002, AARP had thirty-six million members, but apparently they didn't have the one they really wanted: me. Nearly every day my mailbox held an invitation to join AARP, with glossy photos of Goldie Hawn or Paul McCartney or Steve Jobs begging me to join them in the joys of being an old-but-still-sexy person. The implication was that if I joined, I would become a hip elder celebrity like my pals Goldie and Paul and Steve.

Even though I knew it wasn't AARP's fault that I was fifty-five, I resented them pointing it out. At a time when I was desperately seeking the Fountain of Youth, they only offered me the Fountain of Direct Mail. I'm afraid that I lost touch with reality and became a little paranoid about collecting the mail. I imagined I saw Paul Newman staking out my mailbox in an unmarked black NASCAR racer. I was afraid Angela Lansbury would jump out from behind the hedge and try to sell me long-term care insurance.

Then one night Jack Nicholson came to me in a dream and pointed out that the only thing stalking me was myself— the specter of me as an old, retired guy lurking in my future. "What you need to do," Jack said, toasting me with his highball, "is get over yourself."

So after receiving fifty or sixty dollars' worth of direct mail, I finally succumbed and sent in my twenty-five dollars to join AARP. But that didn't stop the direct-mail barrage. Every day there seemed to be some new communiqué from my soul mates at AARP, including more offers to join up, as if AARP had Alzheimer's and had forgotten I already joined. I don't know how they make money this way. They must follow the same economic principle as Laurel and Hardy in an early one-reeler: Stan asks Ollie how they can make money spending three dollars to make a bottle of bathtub gin that they sell for two dollars. Ollie explains, "What we lose on each single bottle we'll make up in volume."

Despite AARP's snail-mail excesses and dubious grasp of fiscal matters, every retired person should join up so we don't fall behind the demographic power curve. Statisticians say that seventy-seven million baby boomers will start retiring in big numbers in 2010. We will be huge in politics, a groundswell of Geezer Power, and AARP will be the most powerful lobbying organization in Washington.

Or maybe not. The other day I had an alarming experience when I cleaned out my wallet. I found three AARP membership cards. I had joined AARP three times before I managed to remember that I'd joined and stopped responding to the recruitment mailings. So maybe there aren't thirty-six million members. Maybe it's twelve million members with three cards each.

3. Retirement Myths

According to the myths, when you retire you begin your golden years. You enter an Olympian realm peopled by godlike beings who live a life of leisure and contentment on a plane far above the worries of mere workaday mortals. It's the Garden of Eden, the Land of Oz, a happy pop song that never ends.

All that sounded good to me. But as I got closer to retirement, I developed a peculiar hearing problem. I heard double meanings in everything people said to me about retirement. For example, a coworker said, "Congratulations! I hear you're retiring," and I heard "First dibs on your office." These auditory hallucinations bothered me so much I started writing them down:

What They Said	What I Heard
Relax and enjoy the rest of your life	You're going to die soon
Spend more time with your family	No more escape from your family
Lucky you, no more work hassles	Just money and health worries
You can take some time for yourself	As soon as you do me this one little favor
Good for you!	One less competitor for me!

| You've earned a rest | Resting is all you're good for anymore |
| Nobody deserves it more than you | You have only yourself to blame |

I felt like my Garden had a serpent problem. The Land of Oz had a wicked witch, and she'd put a poison bean in my ear that colored everything I heard with an evil gloss. The happy pop song I usually have playing in my head changed from "Here Comes the Sun" to "Smoke Gets in Your Ears."

My doctor said there was nothing wrong with my hearing, so I went to my cousin Mara, an alternative healer. "Help!" I said. "My golden years have turned to lead." She took one look at me and declared that my aura was the color of a rotten egg-plant. Fortunately, Mara has studied Aurapuncture and can pop dark auras like ripe pimples. All it took to make me good as new again was a little chanting, some ambient music like sonic wallpaper, and three fifty-eight-dollar aromatherapy candles.

I'm fine now. I love it here in my retirement garden. I have my friends Lion and Scarecrow, and I can sit back, relax, and put my ruby slippers up, out of reach of the serpents. I'm so blinded by their silver linings that I can barely see the dark clouds of my retirement. The radio in my head plays nothing but "Don't Worry, Be Happy" over and over. Over and over. Over and over.

4. Timing

From the frying pan of a full-time job, the fire of retirement looks pretty cool. When should you make the jump from envying the retired to envying the employed? This is a complex question, and the answer depends on financial resources, health, spouse, kids, and how seriously your job sucks. In the limited space available to me, it's pretty much impossible to give a meaningful answer to this complex question, so here goes:

When I thought it might be time to retire, I consulted my business partner, a bona fide psychologist. He told me that the recurring thought, "Maybe I could retire," is what cognitive therapists call an *irrational schema,* or in lay terms, *nuts.* He recommended I try a technique called *thought stopping* to counter such nutty thinking. You carry a taser with you at all times, and every time you think, "Maybe I could retire," you give yourself a good jolt. This functions as a negative reinforcement of the thought. If you do this for a couple of years and the thought goes away, you have successfully extinguished the irrational schema, and it is not time for you to retire.

That sounded pretty easy to me and very scientific. I promised to go taser shopping real soon. But I had to ask my friend, "What if thoughts of retirement persist?" Then, he explained, you add *thought replacement* to your arsenal of sanity: make up four short affirmations and have them tattooed on your forearms and calves. When retirement thoughts arise, roll up your sleeve or pull up your pant leg to read replacement thoughts such as:

You can't afford it.

What would you do all day?

Bad idea.

You're just kidding yourself.

Well, I always wanted a tattoo, and although these weren't as cool as a winged skull, they were medical in nature and therefore deductible expenses on my income tax. If admiring my new tats didn't stop retirement thoughts, the final, surefire technique to try was *thought control:* every time you think about retirement, lock yourself in the bathroom with a boom box, take off all your clothes, and keep yourself awake with cold showers and loud rock music for seventy-two hours.

According to my pal the psychologist, thoughts of retirement that continue to plague you after all these proven interventions are probably legitimate cognitions and a fairly reliable sign that you should retire soon. And he was right. By the time I was done with the taser and the tattoos and the cold showers, I needed to quit work so I could recover from neurological damage, blood poisoning, and pneumonia.

Because the decision about when to retire is so difficult, less psychologically sophisticated people often compromise by retiring from one job and taking another, part-time position. A Gallup poll says 85 percent of retirees continue working after retirement. An AARP poll puts the number at 80 percent. The 5 percent discrepancy is caused by minimum-wage jobs in the service industry that pollsters can't decide whether to call employment or volunteer work.

5. Financial Planning

I got my first financial-planning lesson from my mom, who gave me a piggy bank so I could save my pennies for a rainy day. But I kept them in my pocket and spent every one on licorice whips and peppermints. Later Mom opened a savings account for me, but my core strategy remained the same. I kept my dollars in my wallet and spent them on comics and peppermints. When I got my first full-time job, a personnel lady who looked remarkably like my mom asked me how much of each paycheck I wanted to sock away for retirement. I thought she was kidding. I needed movie tickets and peppermints today, not in the far-distant future.

Eventually I started saving for retirement, but like most folks, it was too little, too late. But my problem wasn't lack of financial planning. Financial *planning* is easy. Everything I needed to know would have fit into a Chatty Cathy doll, one that looks like Ben Bernanke, Head of the Fed. When you pull the ring on Bantering Ben's back, he would say:

Start saving for retirement early.

Balance your portfolio.

Take the long view.

High gain means high risk.

The real problem was financial *achievement*. That's the hard part. From age five I knew it was smarter to put the penny into the pig instead of peppermints. I just couldn't do it until my forties.

Now that my wife, Nancy, and I are in our sixties, financial planning involves adjusting our lifestyle so that we don't end up at age ninety-five living on krill and crackers in a cardboard box. Before I retired, we would occasionally dine at Chez Panisse in Berkeley or spend a weekend at a B&B in the wine country. Now when we want to go someplace expensive, we go to the gas station.

My more spiritually evolved friends tell me that rich and poor are a state of mind, that the secret of prosperity is manifesting riches by thinking positive thoughts. To test this theory we went to the movies yesterday afternoon and instead of paying for our tickets I said, "Let us in free, because I'm rich in mind."

The slender young woman behind the bulletproof glass flipped her blue hair and said, "No way."

"Really," I insisted, "I have put it out to the universe that I'm rich. I'm manifesting two free tickets right now."

She sighed loudly, fiddled with her nose ring, looked right past me and my cosmic mindset, and screeched, "Next!"

I paid for the tickets, but I wasn't discouraged. My friends say it takes time. After the movie, Nancy and I went out for Mexican food. At the end of the meal, our check came with *three* peppermints instead of the usual two.

"At last," I thought. "It's starting to work."

6. Darwin's Joke

Sometimes I feel out of place in the twenty-first century. It reminds me of a movie I saw once where a caveman time travels to the present. He freaks out when he sees cars and TV and stuff. It starred what's-his-name and that actress with the big hair. It was directed by, um, that other guy. Anyway, it'll come to me. My point is that *we are all cavepeople*. We all live in a science-fiction future, but our bodies and minds are still back in the Stone Age.

For millions of years humans lived in small, nomadic tribes, wore fur, hunted and gathered their food, had babies early, and died about two weeks after their babies were old enough to fend for themselves. Then some genius invented agriculture, and we settled into villages, wore homespun fabrics, and grew enough surplus food to live to a ripe old age of thirty-five. We barely had ten thousand years to get used to that, and another genius invented the steam engine. Since then the pace has picked up alarmingly, and in the blink of an eye we had townhouses, spandex, and retirement.

Evolutionary biologists say that our physical and cultural environment has changed too suddenly and drastically for natural selection to keep up. There simply have not been enough generations to evolve the kind of human who is really suited to modern life: presumably one with a built-in cell phone, butt calluses, and an immune system that doesn't go toes-up after age forty.

When you're retired you truly realize how unsuited you are for survival. I'm thinking of getting a tattoo on my forehead: "Surplus Specimen: Too old to bear or rear children, too weak to defend the tribe, freakish byproduct of medical breakthroughs and the welfare state." Kind of verbose as tattoos go, but it will make me look hip, and I have a lot of forehead to cover. If inked in gray italic, it might even look like hair from a distance.

Darwin's joke is that our increased lifespan is actually the booby prize of evolution. Fortunately, there are ways to cope in an environment and at a time of your life when you really should be dead. When faced with a retirement challenge, ask yourself, "What would Fred Flintstone do?" For example, I no longer work in our garden. I have reverted to hunting and gathering whatever happens to be in other people's gardens.

Whenever my offspring make me feel like a surplus specimen, I immediately try to prove myself still useful to the tribe. I grab the nearest grandchild and say to its parents, "Why don't you guys go to the movies tonight and let me babysit this little genius? We'll see what's in the garden and pick some healthy veggies for dinner." When the middle generation has left, me and the grandkid hunt and gather some popcorn and watch that caveman movie again.

7. Working Forever Is Not an Option

One way to avoid retirement problems is to work forever. Unfortunately, that is not really an option—not because older workers are any less efficient than young punks, but because American employers are prejudiced against maturity. They make inflammatory remarks like, "Would you hire a ninety-year-old airline pilot? Quarterback? Sexual surrogate?" This is so unfair. Many jobs, if not most, can be handled perfectly well by oldsters: U.S. senator, political pundit, talk-show host, psychiatrist, Wal-Mart greeter.

That said, even the cushiest sinecure will become tedious eventually. Even workaholics at some point start experiencing the signs that maybe it's time to retire:

- You get the Sunday blues when contemplating the coming workweek.

- Work isn't as sa tisfying or exciting as it used to be.

- They change your office lock and don't give you a new key.

My Uncle Joe was having trouble easing into retirement from the Post Office, so he called me up for some advice. I consulted my collection of old self-help books and came up with the suggestion that he try using affirmations. I explained that affirmations are short little mantras that you recite to yourself. I told him that his affirmations should remind him that he can't work forever, that he deserves some fun, that he is a valuable human being apart from his job, that there are some real advantages to retirement, and so on. I advised him to retreat to a private place whenever he felt nervous about retirement, get comfortable, and recite his affirmations while visualizing a happy retirement.

I guess I should have been a little more specific. Uncle Joe locked himself in a storage closet at work, stripped off all his clothes, and began reciting his affirmations in a loud voice that could be heard throughout the Post Office:

Working forever is not an option.

I can accept this and retire gracefully.

I need more time for my gerbil breeding hobby anyway.

My self-worth does not depend on my job.

In fact, I'm better than 99 percent of these morons.

So what if they throw me out like garbage.

Screw them!

I'll show them!

I'll make them sorry they ever knew me!

As his supervisor removed the closet door from its hinges, Uncle Joe imagined himself leading a carefree retired life, enjoying ample leisure time and exciting new activities, while his ex-colleagues slaved away, occasionally finding the gerbil droppings he planned to leave behind in the mail sacks and file drawers.

8. Living on a Fixed Income

I don't know why they call it a "fixed" income. It looks broken to me. For most of my life I've earned a little more each year. Suddenly I'm retired, and my income is frozen at what I made twelve years ago. When this stark truth became apparent to me, I went to see a financial planner. The first thing she told me was "Never dip into your capital," and I had to ask, "What's capital?" Turns out it's just a fancy term for all your money, which she offered to manage for me at a cost of 1 percent per year.

I declined her offer, even though 1 percent of not much is nearly nothing. I went to see my Uncle Boris, who has been getting along on Social Security for years and is willing to give me all the free advice I can sit still for. He made me a nice cup of hot water and explained that not all my sources of income would be fixed. Social Security occasionally gives out a COLA—Cost-Of-Living Adjustment. But when he looked at my numbers, he said a COLA wouldn't help—I needed straight scotch.

Scotch made me think of my friend Ida. She lives a lavish retired lifestyle, although the only job I remember her holding down was dog walking. When I called her up and asked how she did it, she said, "Not over the phone!" We met in the park by a noisy fountain, and she pointed out that where we live (in northern California), 8 percent of all grandmothers supplement their Social Security checks by growing hydroponic marijuana in their kids' old bedrooms—the real reason they don't want the kids moving back home.

I wasn't quite ready for a life of crime, so I drove home and had a serious discussion with my wife, Nancy, about our finances. We did this exercise from the AARP magazine:

1. Write down your annual retirement income.

2. Subtract all your likely annual expenses.

3. If the remainder is a positive figure, that's your reserve against catastrophic surprises.

4. If the remainder is a negative number, that's the catastrophic surprise.

With our catastrophic surprise looming before us like the federal deficit, we resolved to follow AARP's suggestion and cut expenses. We figured we could cut out cream in our coffee, sugar in our tea, and batteries in the smoke detectors. We could possibly replace expensive hobbies like polo with cheaper activities like bird-watching, except we don't play polo. We could economize on food by dining on free samples at Costco. Instead of paying for expensive dry cleaning or going out to the movies, we could sniff cleaning fluid at home and spend hours watching the dryer go around.

The brainstorming was dampening my spirits, so I took a break. I went out back to collect the eggs. Even the chickens seemed better off than me—they had lots of nest eggs, whereas my nest egg would embarrass a hummingbird.

9. Returning to Work

Don't send your work clothes to Goodwill just yet. We baby boomers can't all retire at once, even if we could afford it. We are the only ones who know how to unjam the copier, how to jiggle the handle on the hydroelectric dam, and how to fiddle the state sales-tax return so the firm won't be audited ... again ... maybe.

One thing that might save many industries from the retiring boomer brain drain is the addictive nature of work. The first time I retired from publishing, it was like quitting nicotine or caffeine. I knew that getting away from the stress of office life was good for me, but sometimes I missed the stimulation. Then they called me up. They had an interesting project that was right down my alley. Could I just help them out with this one little book? In a moment of weakness, I gave in to my cravings for stimulation and slipped back into the work habit for one more hit. I did the project and told myself that it was like tapering off from a beneficial but habit-forming drug. I'd work a while longer, part time and at a slower pace, then quit later—for good.

My mentor in returning to work was my Uncle Cyrus. He retired early from his engineering job at a nuclear power plant then almost immediately went back to work at his old job, earning twice the salary.

"When you go back to work," he advised me, "call yourself a *consultant*."

"But I hate consultants," I said. "A consultant is someone who borrows your watch to tell you what time it is."

"I've told that joke myself," Uncle Cy said. "But when you *are* a consultant, you *love* consultants. You talk about the clarity and objectivity an outside perspective can bring. You bill by the nanosecond and round everything up to next week. As someone with both long experience and fresh perspective, you are a double threat, the most insufferable being possible in any organization: an insider who is also an outsider."

I'm not sure I want to follow Uncle Cyrus's example to the bitter end. His bosses at the nuclear power plant dragged him out of retirement nine times to solve pesky problems with cooling and alarm systems on the aging reactor. He got totally burnt out, but they wouldn't let him quit for good. In desperation, he became a whistle-blower, exposing enough safety violations to the Atomic Energy Commission that they had to shut the reactor down. These days, Uncle Cy is finally enjoying full retirement in the Witness Protection Program. We call him Uncle John now.

10. Retirement School

The other night I sat up late in bed, snacking on trail mix and orange juice in an effort not to eat ice cream and cookies. Nancy was away visiting her mom, so I had all the bills spread out on her side of the bed. I was trying to figure out how to stretch our fixed income to cover the steadily rising costs of taxes, insurance, medications, and trail mix. It was like trying to cram the four horsemen of the apocalypse into a two-man pup tent.

About midnight I gave up, ran my raisiny fingers through my thinning hair, brushed the coconut flakes off the pillow, and turned out the light. When I finally got to sleep I had a nightmare.

I boarded a black school bus full of strangers, old people who all knew each other, knew where we were going, and were infinitely hipper and more clued-in than I was. I couldn't find my bus pass. I had the wrong color Pee Chee folder. My new pencil box was cracked. I had a Hopalong Cassidy lunch box, and everyone else had laptops and briefcases.

We arrived at the Retirement School, a cross between a second-rate junior college and a pretty nice prison. It was in the Mojave Desert, behind a ten-foot chain-link fence with razor wire, guard towers, and a parking lot full of golf carts and motorized wheelchairs.

Even though it was my first day, I was already registered for a bewildering load of courses, each held in widely separated buildings at conflicting times. I dashed from class to class, always late, always in the wrong room.

Philosophy class was the same boring lecture on the Stoics, over and over. History was all genealogy. Science was the chemistry of heartburn and acid reflux. English Lit was like my cousin's reading group—all gossip and no discussion of the book, which was okay because I hadn't read it. When I went to the library, all they had was 200,000 copies of the Reader's Digest Condensed Book version of *The Bridges of Madison County*, large-print edition.

In Economics we played a version of Monopoly called "Downwardly Mobile." You start owning hotels on several monopolies, which you sell for money to live on, buying worse and worse real estate in cheaper and cheaper neighborhoods. The winner is the last player still solvent, squatting in a shack on Baltic Avenue.

Suddenly it was finals week, and I had not even attended some of my required classes.

I woke up trembling, sunflower seeds pasted to my clammy cheek, relieved that it was just a dream. Shaken and weak, I turned on the lights and tottered out to the kitchen.

I felt lots better after some ice cream and cookies.

11. Paperwork

Technology gave us the horseless carriage, the cordless phone, and the wireless Internet connection, but whatever happened to the paperless office? It recedes on the horizon like a mirage in the desert. It's a big lie, like painless dentistry. When I told the human resources priestess that I wanted to retire, she said, "I have a few papers for you to sign," which in HR-Speak means, "Prepare for carpal tunnel syndrome."

I had to fill out forms telling them when I wanted to pull the plug, why I was abandoning ship, what to do with my 401(k) pittance, and where I had filed certain embarrassing e-mails from the CEO. There were a zillion health insurance forms to sign in blood so that my HMO could continue to deny my claims with no break in coverage. An HR acolyte asked me, "Do you want to COBRA?" and I said, "No thanks, I don't dance." I thought it was like the mambo.

At home I had to dig out my latest Social Security statement showing that if I retired early I'd get fourteen dollars per month and my toes would fall off. When I started drawing money out of old IRAs and the 401(k), my tax status changed and these funds had to be reflected in how I filled out my income tax return. Stuff I had been getting away with for years no longer applied, and I had to visit my local IRS Service Center. They gave me such a huge stack of paper that I asked, "What about the Paperwork Reduction Act? What about saving some trees?" and they said, "Sure, we got a form for that."

The wasteland of paperwork made me so grumpy that I lost my way for a while. I started using different middle initials at random. Nobody noticed. Emboldened, I started listing my former occupations as "Astronaut," "Spy," "Nobel Laureate," and "Turkey Sexologist." Nobody even blinked. On a credit card application I used a black magic marker to blank out all the fields having to do with my life in the eighties. When they asked me about it, I said, "Sorry, that's classified." I got the card, but it had an awfully low limit.

Once I played stupid smartass:

Date: No thanks, I'm married.
Address: Of course not! I wear pants, not a dress.
Zip. Oops, sorry … Thanks.
Sex. No way. See "Date," above.

I finally gave up the paperwork games when I checked both "Male" and "Female" boxes on a health-history form. A nurse, a nice older woman, queried me about it, and I got all teary-eyed and said, "It's so confusing when you're born one way but feel another way inside." She teared up too and said, "I know just what you mean. I gave my grandson money for her sex change surgery." I felt ashamed and decided to go back to filling out forms carefully, completely, and honestly.

PART 2

Filling the Empty Hours

12. The Leisure Fallacy

Leisure is the booby prize of retirement. Homeless people, prisoners, and lunatics have leisure. Bimbo heiresses have leisure. Idle pothead trustafarians have leisure. Real people have stuff to do. They are way too busy for leisure. Leisure is a four-letter word with three excess, wasteful letters that offend my Puritan-work-ethic ears. I was raised by working-class parents who considered idle hands the Devil's workshop and no help keeping the grass mowed.

The phrase "free time" is two more four-letter words. In retirement there's altogether too much free time, and it's not free at all. It costs. It costs you by draining your energy and emotional capital. It costs you by mocking your feeble attempts to fill it. Try this exercise: sit up straight in a chair, hands flat on your thighs, legs uncrossed, eyes closed. Do nothing and think nothing for five minutes.

Okay, I know you didn't try it. Readers of self-help almost never do the exercises. That's why they don't get better and we can sell them another self-help book next year. However, in this case you are right not to do the exercise, because it's a setup. It's just meant to show you how impossible it is to think and do nothing. For a few seconds you think, "This is stupid and boring. I must be doing it wrong." Then your mind moves on to thinking about something interesting, worrying about your retirement, brooding over your bills, and so on.

They say time is money. Not true. For the retired, time is the enemy. If you don't creatively fill up your time, it will weigh heavily on your hands. If you have nothing in particular to do, you'll get depressed. Then nothing at all will seem worth doing, and you'll spiral down the drain of leisure.

Your human nature wants you to fill your time with interesting and meaningful thoughts, feelings, and activities. But when you retire, you no longer have a job to fill your time. You have to come up with new stuff to do at a point in your life when you are poorly equipped for the task. You have less money, less energy, and less ability to learn new things. To make matters worse, at this critical juncture when you're vulnerable and confused, some idiot is bound to advise you to just "Take it easy."

There's nothing easy about taking it easy. The first day of my retirement I took it easy for about forty-five minutes. I started reading a 900-page novel I'd been meaning to get to for years. Fell asleep on page nine and woke up half an hour later feeling guilty as hell. I dreamed I'd missed the deadline for filing my quarterly expense report and forgotten for two weeks to feed the dog, who was lying dead on the kitchen floor. To recover, I had to justify my existence by re-grouting all the tile in the bathroom.

13. Pets

Last month our old calico cat, Sophie, died after a lingering illness, and the raccoons ate our last laying hen. I swore off pets for good. They tie you down, exhaust your energy, tax your patience, destroy your stuff, cost a fortune in vet bills, then die and break your heart.

Just when I was comfortable with my decision, I read that researchers have found that retired people with pets live longer. "No," I could have told them, "it just seems longer." In my opinion, those researchers have a lot of nerve. Who authorized them to research pets when they still haven't found a cure for cancer, AIDS, or global warming? Was it our tax dollars at work? Were they secretly financed by the pet lobby?

Apparently if you are over fifty-five and retired, not having a pet is tantamount to suicide these days. So you'd better get a pet before the sheriff breaks down your door and manacles you to a court-mandated animal companion. At least you will have the illusion of choice.

What kind of pet should you get? According to the pet lobby, cats and/or fish are the least trouble, but nothing adores you like a dog. My Uncle Mortimer has a Border collie named DMZ. She's a fine dog, but she sheds her weight in hair each week and her bark is so shrill it pierces your eardrum like an ice pick. All this doesn't matter to Mort, since he's too near-sighted to see the hair on the rug and is too deaf to hear DMZ bark. The moral is to find a pet that is compatible with your deficiencies.

If you're of retirement age, you remember Pet Rocks. They don't count to fulfill your minimum daily pet requirement. Neither do those Japanese virtual pets that live in your computer and eat terabytes of PuterChow. They are too technical and not enough trouble. They develop bugs then die and cause you an effete kind of cyber guilt that is not the true heartbreak you want out of a pet.

Robot pets offer some promise. My cousin Rudy has a Roomba robot vacuum cleaner named Rover. It roves around like a dog, makes a pleasant purring noise like a cat, cleans up instead of dirtying the house, feeds itself from a wall socket, and can be turned off when Rudy goes away. However, when Rover died he was replaced under warranty with an identical model, a very unpetlike outcome.

I think the pet lobby has been tampering with my mind, because I've started to gravitate toward those cardboard boxes full of kittens in front of the grocery store, and I catch myself wondering if the spring chicks have arrived at the feed store yet.

14. Cheap Things to Do

The secret of enjoying yourself on a shoestring is simple. Just take something you do anyway and turn it into a fun game, a creative art form, or an absorbing hobby. The Japanese are great at this, living as they did for centuries confined to one tiny set of islands. They turned ordinary things like rice paper, tea, and tin cans into origami, the tea ceremony, and Toyota.

I like to think of my retirement as a Zen cruise ship and myself as the activities director. I formalize my everyday activities, making each routine a ritual that ennobles common practice and imbues my ordinary behavior with the flavor of a religion or philosophy. I didn't realize this until I was absorbed in buttering my toast one day and Nancy said, "For Pete's sake, it's not the Mona Lisa. Just eat it."

It helps to give your new obsessions special names. Here are some of my favorites:

GAMES

Socko!: Hunting for all the unmatched socks; hint: try under the sofa cushions and inside the arms of the bathrobe you never wear

Nonopoly: Chasing grandkids around, saying "No-no"

Trivial Hirsutes: Fishing hairballs out of the shower drain

ART FORMS

Signography: Driving around, reading signs out loud; try kooky accents for variety

Modern Dunce: Staring blankly at your frozen computer

Skullpture: Combing hair over baldness

HOBBIES

Philintaly: Collecting dryer lint; displays nicely on felt boards, available wherever kindergarten supplies are sold

Dosaics: Sorting your medications and making pill-bottle mosaics

Spellurking: Looking over your spouse's shoulder to correct spelling

SCIENCES

Seasonomy: Alphabetizing and indexing your spices

Garagraphy: Cleaning out the garage

Fizzics: Having another drink

15. More Time Together, Stage One

The cliché is like a *Simpsons* episode: Homer retires and starts hanging around the house, interfering with Marge's routine and driving her crazy. Marge encourages him to find an interest that gets him out of the house. He goes to Moe's Bar, meets a rock 'n' roller voiced by Bruce Springsteen, and becomes a roadie with a band. By the time they cut to the last commercial, Marge has to pose as a gum-cracking groupie to get him out of jail and drag him home.

Could this kind of thing happen to you? Of course not—reality's not like that. Reality is worse. Real retirement lasts a lot longer than a *Simpsons* episode and could use better writers.

In reality one spouse might joke, "It was bad enough to fix you breakfast and dinner every day. Now you want lunch too." In reality the other might quip, "At work I was the boss, but now I'm a trainee in my own home and you tell me what to do." In reality the jokes fall flat and you're left staring at each other, getting on each other's nerves, wishing you could cut to a commercial. In reality you don't get to go on the road with Bruce. You just fight and make up, try this, try that, adjust to each other's maddening ways, and eventually find a compromise lifestyle that pleases neither but keeps you from killing each other.

If you find yourself underfoot, don't despair. There are things you can do. You can add magic to your home life by making yourself disappear from time to time. Take the dog for a walk. Take the car for a wash. Visit your old work and bother them for a while. Remember that everyone, even your spouse, needs some personal space. About a mile is good. If you pester your spouse, you risk starting a border dispute in which you paint a line down the middle of the living room, run dueling TVs at top volume, and need a visa to visit the bathroom.

If your spouse is stalking you, remember that everyone needs and deserves a little privacy. Find someplace you can stake out as your "Alone Place." Hopefully it won't be the only bathroom in the house. Many find their car or garden a refuge. One woman I know liked to retire to her walk-in closet and practice the accordion. When she was in polka mode, her husband knew better than to ask her, "Where's the remote?" or "Could you make me a cup of coffee?"

16. More Time Together, Stage Two

When my cousin Lorelei retired, her husband, Roger, said her personality changed. She seemed more demanding, more moody, more in his face. She couldn't tell him funny stories about the people at work. She no longer went on overnight business trips, leaving him free to eat Ben & Jerry's for dinner with his bare feet up on the coffee table, watching basketball on TV with the sound up loud. He felt that an alien life form had taken over his wife, and he wanted the old Lorelei back.

Dual-career couples sometimes have it easier when they retire at the same time. When my Uncle Jake and Aunt Miriam retired, she said, "It's kind of fun—like meeting someone new and moving in together to set up house ... without the hot sex."

The key to surviving more time together is buried in the middle of the preceding chapter, where I said that newly retired couples "try this, try that." Rather than accept the status quo, you need to use your imagination to keep trying this and that:

- Take up new hobbies.

- Attend local events.

- Join clubs.

- Put the dog in a kennel and travel.

- Get a dog and stay home.

- Try couples' therapy to resolve your pet issues.

- Exercise.

- Meddle more in your kids' lives.

- Dine out.

- Dine in.

- Go on a diet.

The "this and that" you try should include things to do together and things to do separately. You need to balance alone time and together time. Miriam and Jake decided to spend more time together *and* more time separated by getting more involved with their daughter's family. Miriam goes off shopping and on errands with their daughter every Tuesday and Thursday. Jake goes on his own to pick up the grandkids from school on Mondays, Wednesdays, and Fridays. He babysits them at their house, making popcorn and watching DVDs until the daughter gets home from work. On Sundays, Jake and Miriam go together to have dinner at their daughter's house. This all worked very well until their daughter asked them to "*Please*, get a life of your own."

You need to be patient with each other. Mistakes will be made. One man had his hearing aid turned off when his wife said she wanted to try sushi. He thought she said "slushy," so he took her to 7-Eleven. It turned out okay—it seems that sushi and slushies go remarkably well together.

17. Your Shrinking Key Ring

My Uncle Jack "the Flipper" Price made a modest bundle in real estate, but his doctor told him he'd better slow down for his arteries' sake. When Uncle Jack retired, he surrendered the keys to his old office, street door, company car, storeroom, safe, and various lockboxes. He handed over the keys to his lake house in Tahoe to the new, younger, and more solvent owners. His social circle contracted so that fewer people gave him keys to feed their cat or water their plants. It really hurt when his girlfriend asked for her keys back because her self-image could not sustain intimacy with a retired person.

I, too, have experienced key-ring shrinkage in retirement, but I like to think of it as simplifying my life. I've escaped the onerous responsibilities of gainful employment and an active, involved lifestyle. No longer weighed down with six pounds of keys, I feel light as a feather, free as a bird, detached as a Zen monk, a convict, or a homeless person.

Since keys were on my mind when I retired, I decided to sort through and organize the flotsam and jetsam of "mystery keys" that had washed up on the shores of my life over the years. I collected all the extra keys from the kitchen junk drawer, the garage junk drawer, the family-room junk drawer … well, all our drawers are junk drawers, so I went through every one and pulled out all the keys I could find.

I ran around trying every key in every lock and realized that we had five different locks on five different house doors. Back when I was working, I would have shrugged this off as just another symptom of a complicated, stressful, and illogical life.

But now that I'm retired, I have the time to iron out these little wrinkles in the bunched undies of my existence.

I removed all the door locks and took them to a locksmith. He keyed all the locks alike, so that one key would open all five doors, and I returned home with new keys for everybody. I labeled and color-coded every currently active key. I ended up with thirty-one useless keys, including the key to my bike lock in seventh grade, the key to my mom's '62 Rambler, and the key to the suitcase we lost on our honeymoon to Mexico in 1982.

Just in case, I tried every key in every lock again. When I was absolutely certain that none of the keys was important, I put them all back in the junk drawer. You never know—that suitcase may turn up someday.

By this time it was dark, and I was exhausted. I made a sandwich and sat down to watch a movie. That's when I noticed the TV was gone.

18. Going Through Things

The first sixty years are all about acquisition. My first apartment was furnished by dumpster diving. I was a traffic menace, driving through San Francisco with one eye on the sidewalk for dumpsters or unwanted items left out on trash night. I would double park and hold up an irate bus driver if it meant scoring a spavined kitchen chair from the fifties.

Later, I actually paid for things, first at thrift stores and garage sales, then moving up to Cost Plus and Sears. Then I discovered that when you get married, they give you more stuff than you could ever afford on your own, so I did that a couple of times. And in the last few years, eBay has allowed me to dive in the global dumpster without ever leaving home. Now I get not only the $500 collectable fifties kitchen chairs, but the ton of cardboard they are shipped in.

Periodically I moved, mostly to get more space to put stuff in. By the time I was sixty, we lived on two acres in the country, with a house and a barn and a four-car garage. "Are there four cars in the garage?" you might ask. No—it's too full of bikes and pianos and fifties dinette sets. The six cars are parked outside. That's why we need two acres.

This is all very embarrassing for me, especially since I consider myself a pseudo-Buddhist and once wrote half a book about how to simplify your life. Obviously the second sixty years must be about divestiture. Thank God I'm retired and have the time to go through things.

I was amazed to discover that we owned thirty-eight vases and six ice-cream scoops, although I have no memory of ever personally acquiring a single vase or scoop.

First I thought that we'd have a garage sale the next weekend. But I looked at the calendar and the next sixteen weekends were booked with essential retirement activities: visit my dad; visit Nancy's mom; help our son move into his new house; the Apple Blossom Festival; the Strawberry Festival; the Harvest Festival; a jazz concert; a film festival; another financial planning seminar; etc., etc.

Then I figured out that I should just give things away. My son was moving into a new house and needed lots of stuff. He didn't have room for a piano, but I got him to agree to take a dinette set and a couple of his old bikes. I loaded them into the trailer and headed on over. He was having a housewarming party, so I stopped on the way to pick up some ice cream and flowers, which naturally required the purchase of a nice vase and an ice-cream scoop. Well, he's got forty years before he has to worry about going through things.

19. The Switcheroo

Many retired couples trade household chores. He starts doing the laundry or watering the house plants. She starts paying the bills or taking out the trash. But some couples radically reverse their roles, a maneuver known as the Switcheroo.

For example, my Uncle Bert was an engineer who worked for years in Arizona designing large irrigation systems that his wife, Laura, a committed Sierra Club member, blamed for depleting the aquifer and raising soil salinity. She once testified at a Water Board hearing in opposition to one of Bert's projects. Then Bert retired and took up yoga and meditation. Laura became a county supervisor and helped plan the redevelopment of the neighborhood where Bert's ashram was located. He ended up picketing Laura's office, protesting the redevelopment: Switcheroo.

Gender barriers crumble for retired persons contemplating a Switcheroo. If you're a woman, it is okay to rebuild a classic motorcycle, open a hardware store, or take boxing lessons. If you are a man, it's okay to attend pilates classes, wear pink, or sew quilts. Late in life, men often take up cooking and spend more time in the garden. They become more detached, spiritual, and inward looking. At the same time, many older women take up golf or power walking and spend more time in outward-looking activities like volunteer or club work. They start businesses and run for office.

Perhaps we are becoming more Asian. In India there is a tradition of older men retiring and then leaving their wives to move into a monastery to become monks. Their wives are then free to turn their houses into textile cooperatives, electronic assembly lines, and call centers.

This is sort of what happened when another aunt and uncle of mine pulled a Switcheroo. Aunt Maybelle tried for years to get Uncle Herb to stop going to the dog races, where he would gamble away her earnings from her beauty parlor and come home smelling of greyhound and peppermint schnapps. Late in life Herb converted to the AA religion, with a minor in Gamblers Anonymous. He began speaking almost entirely in bumper stickers. He joined Greyhound Rescue, filling their apartment with arthritic racing dogs and haranguing Maybelle about the beauty products she sold that were tested cruelly on animals. She finally cancelled all her appointments and used the parlor exclusively to deal OxyContin and run numbers.

So don't worry if something you want to do reminds you of your spouse. Don't worry if it's too weird or conventional, too feminine or masculine, too liberal or conservative. Be grateful that you're still interested in something, and just pull a Switcheroo.

20. Turn Your Hobby into Extra Income

I like to restore old pianos. They are made entirely of simple, renewable materials like wood, felt, steel, and glue—no plastic to crumble or computer chips to become obsolete and fail. The piano is one of the great achievements of human ingenuity. It is the height of nineteenth-century industrial design, a design that has not been significantly improved for over a hundred years.

One of my cool ideas for retirement was to turn my piano hobby into a source of extra income. I envisioned myself working meditatively in the barn, regulating the action on a gleaming grand piano, classical music tinkling on the radio, a cup of tea on the workbench. I would work only for friends who appreciated fine instruments and had the patience to wait for me to do it right.

The only bad thing about pianos is that hardly anybody needs more than one, and all my musical friends already had one. Well, there's actually a second bad thing: pianos take up a lot of space. Some of my friends were moving into smaller houses and replacing their pianos with electronic keyboards. Oh, and a third bad thing is that pianos are heavy and expensive to move. So when my friends gave me their orphan pianos, I had to pay the movers. My extra-income hobby became a source of extra expense. And my wife, Nancy, was not happy about having to park her car outside because a grand piano needed the garage.

Finally I heard that my local art center needed a grand piano, so I promised them one of mine as soon as it was restored.

They couldn't afford to pay, so this would be a donation. But at least I could work on an instrument that was going to a good home. Unfortunately, when I looked closely at the pianos I had access to, none was ideal. So I went around to local piano stores and found a repairable 1923 Mason & Hamlin that the store owner was willing to let go for cheap, and he'd throw in an 1894 Chickering for nothing! All I had to do was pay for the moving.

I nearly destroyed my lungs putting a glossy black finish on the Mason & Hamlin, and I was so rushed I didn't have time for many tea breaks. But it was worth it when I heard it played in concert last spring by a real virtuoso. It sounded great and made me realize that you can turn your hobby into emotional income, if not the financial kind.

Now if I could just get the Chickering out of the garage and Nancy's car back in.

21. Polishing Your Tarnished Years

After a few years of retirement, my Uncle Edgar's golden years became tarnished. He was bored to death with his hobbies, his children, and his grandchildren. His health was failing faster than he wanted, and Aunt Osiris, never the liveliest woman, was hanging around his neck like a dead albatross. He felt so used up and useless that he was ready for the final solution, the ultimate degradation, the last refuge of the desperate: volunteer work.

For Edgar, volunteering was like flossing his teeth—supposedly good for you, but who could possibly enjoy it? He couldn't understand how work that was drudgery when done for pay could be pleasure when done for free.

I reminded him of my cousin Sven, who broke out in hives doing software design for IBM, but now looks forward to running the computer system for his local food bank. Plus, there's Aunt Rhonda, the family entrepreneur, who finds cooking the books for a local nonprofit much less stressful and more enjoyable than flimflamming the IRS on her own behalf. She gets to enjoy the familiar thrill of fraud with a much lower risk of prosecution.

Dubious but desperate, Uncle Edgar went down to a busy volunteer center in his town and filled out a lot of aptitude and interest forms. He was told that, with his teaching background, he would be ideal for reading to the blind or tutoring illiterate adults. He agreed to try tutoring, and they set up an appointment for him to visit one of their clients. Edgar was nervous as he rang the bell at the student's house. A pale young man let him into a dim living room. The furnishings were very shabby and the guy's dog was really stinky. But Edgar was game. He turned on some lights and handed the student a book.

"Let me hear you read page five out loud," Edgar said in his most encouraging voice.

The guy stared in his direction blankly for a while, opened the book, looked down, then looked up and shyly said, "You do know I'm blind, don't you?"

This was the funniest thing Edgar had heard since retiring, and it sold him on volunteering. He still reads to that blind guy, and they always start each session with the same joke.

"Told you so," I said to Uncle Edgar when I heard the story. "I was right about volunteering, wasn't I?"

"I suppose. It's like flossing—takes some effort, but it pays off."

"Why did it take you so long to see that?"

"You do know I'm blind, don't you?"

22. How May I Be of Service?

When you are employed, you can see yourself as a contributing member of society because you're holding down a job, earning money, and providing for yourself and your family. When you retire, the question often arises, "How may I be of service now?" As we saw in the last chapter, for some the answer is lots of volunteer work.

My cousin Lily was a psychology professor who agreed with Socrates that the unexamined life is not worth living. She was an introspection junkie, forever looking inward and contemplating her feelings and motivations, pondering the nature and meaning of her Self (with a capital S). By the time she retired, Lily knew every nook and cranny of her psyche and was sick of her precious Self. She decided that the overexamined life wasn't worth living, either. She abandoned her Self and devoted her time to reading books out loud, recording them for the blind. The only books she refused to read were those on psychology.

Do you wake up some days, look in the mirror, and ask, "Who is that?" Does your calendar stretch out before you as a vast and formless void, marked only with the phases of the moon and your dog's birthday? Is the most exciting thing on your horizon clipping your toenails or changing the water in the fishbowl? Have you become boring and useless to yourself? Perhaps it's time to be of use to others. Just don't try to get too creative.

According to some guy on the radio (which is where I get most of my good ideas), creative people find unique volunteer work in contexts where they are already involved, comfortable, and have existing relationships. Since I've always been fond of our mailman, I met him at the mailbox one day in my own letter-carrier outfit of gray shorts, sturdy walking shoes, and a pith helmet.

"Your troubles are over, George," I told him. "I'm going to give you a hand today."

I never knew the postal service had so many picky regulations. Although the FBI people later apologized, and they waived most of the fines, it put me off volunteering for a while.

Even so, I got off easier than my Uncle Bradley, who listened to the same guy on the radio. Bradley asked his favorite bartender what he could do to help. The bartender needed a ride to a lonely rest stop on the state highway, where Bradley helped him unload cases of liquor from a parked truck into his car. The jury had no sympathy for Brad's defense that he was "just a volunteer" in the liquor hijacking.

23. The C Word

Change, like death and taxes, is unavoidable and scary. The essence of change is giving up something old and familiar in favor of something new and unfamiliar. Even if you retire willingly from a job you hate, with enough money and good health and a loving spouse, the change can be stressful. The stress can become overwhelming if you are forced to retire from a job you like, with little money or bad health or a relationship on the rocks. It's like being dumped from a warm bed into icy, shark-infested water.

Too much C word can make you cycle from fear, to anger, to depression, to fear, to anger, to depression, and so on—like a hamster on a wheel going flat-out and getting nowhere. At those times, I've found that the best thing to do is to pause and literally take a breath. Lie down, close your eyes, and take long, slow breaths. Tell yourself:

> It's just change.
> These feelings will pass,
> and I will remain
> a good little hamster—
> I mean person.

Strange as it seems, when you're in hamster mode, at some point during retirement you will go from fearing the C word to craving it—because life without enough change is predictable and boring. Every Sunday you have skinless chicken breasts and sort out a week's worth of pills into that plastic thingy. Every Monday you take out the trash and change the blah

blah. Tuesdays you go to your blah meeting and see blah blah. Wednesdays you blah and blah and more blah. It's like *not* being dumped from tepid, you-infested water.

If you're bored in retirement, consider making a sudden U-turn. Although most people change slowly and gradually, there are exceptions, and maybe you're one of them. Acquiring new habits doesn't have to be slow. Radical, sweeping, instant, 180-degree change can happen to you.

Until I was thirty, I hated cars. They were a necessary evil—expensive, polluting, noisy, mechanically mysterious, and always breaking down at the worst possible moment. Then somebody left a book about classic-car restoration at my house, and I idly picked it up one evening. I stayed up all night reading it. Over the next twenty years I bought, restored, and sold several cars and trucks from the thirties, forties, and fifties. I went from being a car hater to being a stone car guy overnight. I learned about engines and design history and restoration techniques. I did most of the work myself, acquiring many tools and skills. I got years of pleasure from a hobby I used to consider a stupid waste of time. I still haven't gotten all the grease out from under my fingernails.

I like to remember this 180-degree change when I feel bored. I remind myself that I don't have to remain as I am: a sarcastic, snobbish, blue-state man into writing and film and classical music. If I get bored enough, I can become a sincere, gregarious, red-state guy who loves baseball and beer and country music.

Sounds like fun.

24. Travel

In my heart of hearts, I don't particularly like to travel. I'd rather stay home near my dear possessions and in my comfortable routine. If I want the travel experience, I can get it at home by hiding all my clean underwear, sticking rocks under my mattress, and eating too much of food I don't like. However, many active retirees like to travel. They have the time, the energy, and the money—at least until they get home and open the credit-card bills.

I thought I should at least give retirement travel a try, so I signed up for a hiking tour of Croatia. The trip was organized by Elderhostel, an aptly named group. Those people were both old and hostile. One grandma nearly started a new Balkan war because she had to wait seven minutes for a cup of coffee. Another guy who had signed up for a trip advertising "strenuous hiking on steep, rocky, mountain trails" complained constantly about the rocks and his fear of heights.

Okay, I know the difference between "hostel" and "hostile." But I don't think the organization should use the term at all, because nobody ever stays in a hostel. The hotels are four-star establishments, with good-sized rooms, decent restaurants, English-speaking staff, and so on. Nothing at all like a youth hostel, with bunks and sleeping bags and barefoot guys selling hash in the communal bathroom. The hotels are carefully chosen to appeal to older travelers: they have elevators, extra-firm beds, and generous dinner buffets with four kinds of dessert and five types of anti-inflammatories. Elderhostel trips are expensive, dedicated to the proposition that the more you spend on a trip, the larger your hotel room and the less novelty you must endure.

I enjoyed Croatia itself. Except for having more names for coffee, hot water, and milk than Starbucks, it was very unpretentious. We visited a botanical garden that consisted of a scattering of weeds with their Latin names painted on rocks. The visitor center was a padlocked Porta Potti. There was no one around to collect the admission fee, just an iron pipe sunk in concrete with a coin slot hopefully lettered in Croatian, English, and Italian: "Help us. Thank you." I'm thinking of opening one of these botanical gardens in my front yard at home.

From my limited travel experience, I have learned that there are basically two kinds of travelers: the enthusiast who loves everything and the grump who hates everything. To succeed at travel, you should pick your side of this continuum and stay there. Don't confuse people by being wishy-washy, liking some things and not liking others. Be consistent.

Finally, if you pick the grumpy camp, face the fact that you would rather be right than be happy, and stay home.

25. The Permanent Vacation

Some retirees sell their homes, buy recreational vehicles, and embark on a permanent vacation, crisscrossing the land in a constant search for Laundromats, pull-thru parking, and 120-volt hookups. They drift from mountain to shore, from scenic wonder to roadside attraction, from blood relative to in-law, from Disneyland to Disney World.

The RV lifestyle has great appeal to retired couples who want to completely reinvent themselves. They morph from husband and wife into driver and navigator. It seems to be a very patriarchal society in which the men wear the pants and do the driving, and the women choose the trim package and fold the maps. There may be a woman somewhere who drives these things, and a man who can fold a map, but I've never seen either one.

Picking the right recreational vehicle is a function of how much closeness you can tolerate. If togetherness still sounds good, get a self-contained motor home, where the driver is basically sitting in the living room with the passenger. If you prefer more separation, get a pickup and a "fifth wheel," which is essentially what we used to call a trailer but is priced more like a two-bedroom condo. With a fifth wheel, the driver can be up front in the truck and the passenger can be in the back. I think this is illegal in some states, but a moving violation is better than spouse-i-cide. Some incompatible couples roam the earth for years in their fifth wheels, like shark and remora, never stopping, always moving, restlessly alone together.

Some folks are not ready to devolve permanently and completely to a preindustrial, nomadic lifestyle, but they try it for a period of time. They go on what Germans call a *Wanderjahr*—a year of wandering to find themselves or to find where they want to live in their retirement. That's what my Aunt Bettina and her second husband, Hank, did when they sold their auto-recycling yard and retired. Hank made their RV from an old Blue Bird school bus, with a Jaguar engine and interior fitments from a flood-damaged Winnebago. They had several cute names for it, like Jagabago, Winnie-Bird, and the Blue Lagoon.

Hank drove and Bettina folded maps for about a week, and then they broke down for the first time. Hank crawled underneath and Bettina handed him wrenches, which was disturbingly like not being retired anymore. They broke down nearly every week, usually in the middle of nowhere. After about nine months of this, Bettina said they had to settle down, preferably in a big city with lots of auto-parts stores. Finally Hank parked the Jagabago for the last time in Minneapolis, and Bettina took a taxi on to Saint Paul. They still send each other Christmas cards.

PART 3

Lifelong Learning

26. Lifelong Learning

In retirement you are praised for behavior that would have drawn nothing but criticism when you were in your twenties: being a perpetual student. Colleges across the nation are bulging with retired folks taking classes in everything from glass blowing to real-estate development. My local community-college campus looks like a drop-in day-care center for seniors.

I have been taking junior-college classes regularly, sampling art forms and disciplines I had no time for as a youth and for which I have increasingly little aptitude. I was a smarty-pants English major in college who felt offended and threatened by professors who gave me less than an A. Now I can get Cs in Music Theory or Beginning Fencing and shrug them off. What do I care if my transcript reads like the meanderings of a schizophrenic simpleton? I'm not preparing for a career here. I'm just futzing around. I've finally stopped worrying about my "permanent record."

That said, I still like my As, when I can get them, and so do a lot of my older classmates. Younger students hate our guts because we sit in the front row, pay attention, ask questions, and wreck the grading curve. I tell them get used to it: when they get out in the real world, every top job they want will be held down by a curve-wrecking old fogey, so they'd better learn to compete.

A lot of people these days are talking about slow food: shopping for fresh ingredients and cooking slowly and carefully. I'm experiencing slow learning: groping for fresh ideas and thinking slowly and stupidly. For one thing, my brain is older and slower than it used to be. It's harder to grasp new concepts and memorize stuff. In music-theory class I've laboriously memorized and promptly forgotten the circle of fifths for every quiz and midterm so far. Secondly, I'm trying to learn stuff I've always avoided because I don't have a knack for it: reading music, playing the piano, and singing on key. If I were a member of the von Trapp family, they'd put me up for adoption.

My finest lifelong learning experience has been Beginning Fencing. I'm the only old guy in a class of eight, but we have achieved a true meeting of the minds between young and old. I have the experience and the deep historical perspective of someone who has watched Errol Flynn in *Captain Blood* six times. I show the youngsters all the classic pirate and Robin Hood movie tricks. And they, in turn, bring me up to date on the sword-fighting innovations of Jackie Chan, Frodo, and *The Princess Bride*. As we caper around the gym like monkeys, stomping and shouting, decapitating candlesticks, swinging on chandeliers, and circling backwards up tower staircases, our instructor just shakes her head and weeps at the beauty of it all.

27. The Retired Computer

In retirement, I finally mastered Photoshop. I used to sit staring disconsolately at the screen as the program loaded, reading all thirty-nine names of the Adobe programmers who contributed code to Photoshop, imagining that each one of them spent the brightest flame of their youthful intellects perfecting one more feature to keep me from doing what I wanted with the vintage photo of Grandma at Lake Minnetonka.

Once again, the JC came to the rescue. Nancy and I signed up for a Photoshop class taught by a sharp young fellow who also worked at a local photography store. When we enrolled, I was amazed that the course only cost forty-five dollars. Then we went to the first class and found out about the lab fee and the necessity of buying the current iteration of the complete Photoshop software. Seems the version on our computer was a special complimentary edition bundled free with computers purchased by veterans of the Civil War. By the second class we learned about plug-ins—extra filters and effects you can get for ninety-nine dollars a crack. And after the third class, we visited our teacher at his store to pick up a new digital camera. Several hundred dollars later, I was still amazed, but in the other direction.

But it was worth it. We learned how to quickly take the red out of people's eyes, the telephone wires out of sunset skies, and our wallets out of our pockets. I could scan photos from magazines and make the president and the chief justice of the USA look like they were premiering together in *Swan Lake* at Lincoln Center. I even went on the Adobe website and made suggestions for three new features the program lacks: "Muffin

Top," for adding the tops of people's heads you cut off; "Who the Heck?", for identifying strangers in your photos; and "Slimby," for taking off a few pounds in photos where you look fat. Adobe is still working on these.

For our final project, Nancy improved our wedding portrait with a floral background from another photo, better contrast, and softer colors. She's never liked the expression on my face in that shot, calling it my "Grim Reaper" face, whereas I remember being seriously moved by the gravity of the ceremony. It was one of those post-neo-hippie weddings in eighties Berkeley, a potluck affair in a neighborhood park.

Anyway, she replaced my head with one from a photo taken later in the day, when the cheap champagne had mellowed my expression. When she was done, she was delighted with the result. It looked like she had married a completely different guy at a completely different time and place. I love how Photoshop and the retired computer help us preserve our most cherished memories.

28. Become a Brilliant Conversationalist

I went to my fortieth high-school reunion, and I couldn't believe how boring we had all become. The wild kids who had me laughing tuna salad out my nostrils at their antics in the cafeteria were now droning on about property values and medical bills and private schools for their "problem" children. They had gone from being problem children to having their own, and it was boring—like being caught in a ten-hour version of *Night of the Living Fogeys*.

On the plane ride home, I resolved to become a brilliant conversationalist. The lady next to me asked, "What do you do?" and I began practicing on the spot. Instead of saying that I'm retired or I used to be a publisher, I said, "I'm an experienced publisher with twenty-five years of seniority."

Unfortunately, my reluctance to mention the R word launched her on a chapter-by-chapter summary of her cool ideas for a book on the mosses of Greenland, reminding me why I had retired from publishing in the first place.

Despite this setback, I was determined to sparkle conversationally. At a fundraiser the next week, the dreaded "What do you do?" question came up repeatedly, and I did better. I made up impressive titles for how I spend my time now. Trying to get my son to call his grandfather became "social engineering." Begging my insurance company to pay medical bills became "mediation and contract compliance." Scratching off lottery tickets became "statistical analysis." Answering a two-year-old grandson's constant "Why … why … why?" became "consulting." Unfortunately, to back up these boasts, I had to write several checks to Beloved Bovines, a charity I would not normally support so enthusiastically.

Undeterred, I decided to become known as a fascinating conversationalist by avoiding clichéd topics and asking provocative questions instead. When my cousin Bruno asked how my sore hip was doing, I asked him, "If you were the last person left alive on earth, how would you pass your time?"

He said, "Huh?"

"Let me put it this way," I clarified. "If you could only accomplish one more important thing before you die, what would it be?"

"Are you feeling okay?"

"Or how about this?" I said. "Imagine you are given a time machine and you can make one visit to the future. What year would you visit and why?"

Bruno excused himself and went off to confer with my wife, Nancy. A little later she took me aside and suggested that I stop being a wise guy, because people were starting to ask her if I was all right and suggest that I could use a neurological workup.

Brilliance is just wasted on some people.

29. Good Tech/Bad Tech

My neighbor Millie is eighty-seven and suffers from early-stage Alzheimer's. She has macular degeneration and can't read her kitchen clock, wristwatch, or calendar anymore. Her daughter got her a talking clock/calendar that is small enough to carry around in her purse. It has two large buttons. Push one and a pleasant, male, British voice tells you the time. Press the other button and he tells you the date. The clock has a radio-receiver chip in it that regularly checks in with a satellite and resets the time when necessary. It automatically adjusts for daylight savings time and leap years. The lithium battery will last for years. This is good technology for Millie since the interface is simple, the technology is invisible, and it does just what she wants with no upkeep required. If she forgets what it is, she picks it up, pushes a button, and remembers that it's her clock.

My cousin Carl is a retired electrical engineer and gourmet cook. For his seventieth birthday I got him a meat thermometer with a probe that remains in the meat while it cooks. A wire goes out to the counter and plugs into a readout unit that tells him how long his roast has been cooking and what temperature it has reached in the middle. The unit broadcasts to a wireless remote that he can carry in his apron pocket when he goes outside to check on his pit-baking yams. It sounds an alarm when the meat's temperature has reached the "done" stage, which he has programmed to a tenth of a degree for fourteen different kinds of meat, fish, and fowl.

For most people, especially someone like Millie, this thermometer would be bad tech, because it's overkill. You don't really need it. It complicates a basically simple process of heating meat until it tastes good and won't give you parasitic dysentery. But it's good tech for Cousin Carl because it appeals to his engineer's soul. Fiddling with it makes him happy and keeps him sharp.

When you're retired, you have many needs that good tech can help you meet and bad tech can frustrate. For example, e-mail can help you stay in contact with friends and relatives, or it can frustrate that need. If "spam" to you is a breakfast food and "Smiley" was Tex Ritter's horse, then use the phone and send birthday cards by the U.S. Postal Service.

Likewise, the Internet is a revolutionary leap forward in information technology, but if you think of "pop-ups" as something you cook in the toaster, then continue to patronize your library, get your maps from AAA, and give your computer to some techno geek who will actually enjoy using it.

30. Stop Me if I've Told You This

When I retired, my social circle shrank and my charming tendency to repeat the same old stories became a serious character flaw. I was like a basic-cable channel that played only reruns. This is a genetic trait that I inherited from my Aunt Loretta, whose stories are as predictable and invariant as the canon of the Mass. Somebody mentions sick pets, and she launches into "Muffin's Psoriasis." Someone foolishly asks her how she met her husband, and they have to sit through the director's cut of "Forest's Modest Proposal."

People wouldn't mind Loretta's reruns so much if they had a crisp, three-act structure, with a nicely shaped rise and fall of dramatic action and a tidy Hollywood ending. But no. She makes the same false starts, digressions, and non sequiturs every time. As her husband, Forest, says, "Loretta's always got to go all the way 'round the barn to get to the woodshed, and mostly she don't ever get there."

Here is a typical Loretta story: "One time I bet my cousin Lulu she wouldn't kiss a trout. We were in Grandpa Otis's old rowboat, the one he borrowed from Mrs. Ford and never returned after she died. Her old doctor treated her colitis for twenty years, then he retired, and the new, young doctor said it was cancer all along, and she was dead inside a month. Mrs. Ford put up her Christmas decorations and never took them down, just like those lights Harold's boy nailed up on my roof three years ago, and there they are to this day, all rusty and nasty and don't work." No matter how long you listen or how tactfully you try to get her back on track, you'll never find out what happened with Lulu and the trout.

Aunt Loretta retired from being a claims adjuster with Hartford and started doing a lot of volunteer work with Father Mike at Saint Patrick's Church. Instead of telling her stories to a diverse group of policyholders who listened tolerantly in hopes of bilking the Hartford Group out of a settlement, she was boring a relatively small, captive audience of parishioners who wished she would shut up so they could get a word to God in edgewise.

Father Mike asked me to intervene after he had received several complaints about Loretta's loquacious visits to St. Pat parishioners in the local nursing home. He had begun to develop the suspicion that their rising death rate might be attempts to escape Loretta's stories.

Since this problem runs in our family, and so that Loretta wouldn't be singled out, I got the whole family involved. Six of us carried around a pack of three-by-five index cards and monitored our conversations for a month. After telling a story, we jotted down its subject and to whom we told it on a card. When we found that we had repeated the same story to the same person, we put a big red X across that card and stopped telling that story.

At the end of the month, we all got together for dinner and shared our experiences. It was a remarkable event. Six of the gabbiest people on earth spent three hours in silence, taking turns holding up index cards marked with big red Xs.

31. Memory Isn't a Lane, It's a Swamp

Someday, when we all have computers implanted in our medullas, we will have perfect memories. If you're 125 years old, and you can't remember Picasso's name or the word "ergonomic," you will close your eyes and ask your internal search engine for "orthopedic furniture" or "painter of *Guernica*," and the elusive words will pop into your mind. Every conversation will sparkle with specific names and dates and facts, although there will be very little eye contact.

In the meantime, we're stuck with our base-model human memory, wetware that has one unfixable bug: the older you get, the more you have to remember in a brain of finite capacity. They say we only use 10 percent of our brains and the rest is dormant, but I think the other 90 percent is actually doing something, especially in older people. I think it's in charge of forgetting. And the longer you live, the more you have to forget, so more and more brainpower must be devoted to forgetting. This leaves less and less available for remembering—a vicious downward spiral. And that's before you even turn on the TV.

I like to use mnemonics to remember names, although I can seldom remember the word "mnemonic." For example, I associate Mary, a waitress at the local coffee shop, with the Virgin Mary—she has the same sweet smile as the statue in the Catholic church I visited as a boy. I see the smile, think of the statue, and "Mary" pops into my mind. Unfortunately, I also genuflect when she walks by.

Many retirees are afraid of Alzheimer's sneaking up on them, so they do crossword and Sudoku puzzles or sign up for

Introduction to Calculus at the JC. As my Aunt Jinny used to say, they are drawing bears in the window: scaring themselves with a bogeyman they will be too loopy to recognize if it ever does turn up. If you can easily remember the word "Alzheimer's," you don't have it. Even if you sometimes forget the word, but when reminded of it, you realize you knew it all the time, you don't have it. If Alzheimer's is news to you every time someone explains it to you, you have it, but you don't know it—and so it doesn't matter. It's so simple: as long as you're worried about Alzheimer's, you have nothing to worry about. If you're not worried about Alzheimer's, you have nothing to worry about.

Since trips down Memory Lane will increasingly strand you in Memory Swamp, stay out of it. "Be here now," as the Buddhists say. Or as they say in the Alzheimer's ward, "Be here new."

32. Mentoring

When retirement makes me feel stale and useless, I need a way to bring my better self to the surface, like cream rising to the top of milk. In my need to escape myself, I envy the lowly starfish, who can literally get outside of itself by regurgitating its own stomach. At those times I make myself feel better by helping out a younger person. I am a "mentor," which in Greek means "creamy starfish."

In Greek mythology, Mentor babysat Telemachus while his father, Odysseus, was away coining the term "odyssey." Sometimes the goddess Athena took Mentor's form to counsel Telemachus. Since then, wise and trusted advisors have been called "mentors," although they could just as easily have been called "athenas."

In the business world, a mentor is an older executive who helps an aspiring youngster up the corporate ladder, wisely counseling him or her not to step on the mentor's head on the way up. In retirement, a mentor is someone lucky enough to know a younger person who is needy or polite enough to sit still for advice. The younger person is called the "mentoree," which reminds me of "manatee." I think this is an appropriate association, since I see myself as pulling awkward, passive young people out of the way of the deadly propellers on the Motorboat of Life.

My most recent mentoree was my young neighbor Sean, who wanted to quit smoking. Having long ago given up smoking myself, I volunteered to be his mentor. When I showed up at Sean's door on the day he planned to quit smoking, things were in an uproar. Sean's head was in the oven, and his cat, Fizzbang, was prowling back and forth, yowling. It seems that moments before, Sean and Fizzbang had seen a mouse crawl out of a burner hole on their old gas stove. The cat sprang to the top of the stove, scaring the mouse back down inside, and burning her paws on the pilot light. Sean is tenderhearted and didn't want to set a trap to kill the mouse, or let it be caught and eaten by Fizzbang, or even worse, cook it to death in the oven.

I sprang into action. My cool, wise old head came up with the perfect plan: put the cat outside and turn on the gas in the oven, forcing the mouse out the top again. Then we'd suck the mouse up in the vacuum cleaner and take the vacuum bag to the park down the street, releasing the little critter into the wild.

The plan worked perfectly, up to the point where the mouse got stuck in the vacuum hose. We opened a window, reversed the airflow, and shot the mouse out into the back yard like a bullet—straight into Fizzbang's jaws. I ran outside to intervene, but the mouse was history. Sean collapsed into a chair at the kitchen table and lit a cigarette with shaky hands. That's when the stove blew up.

Sean had to move away after his eviction, but he keeps in touch by e-mail. His eyebrows grew back, and he hasn't had a cigarette since, thanks to my mentoring.

33. Become a Wise Elder

I think I like to joke too much to be a wise elder, but the gig is attractive because wisdom earns more respect than jokes and it's fun to give advice. So I went around to the store in town that sells incense and meditation bells and Native American talismans made in China. I sat on a massage chair in the corner and observed how wise elders ply their trade. Here is the list of guidelines I came up with:

BE CRYPTIC

Baffle them with obscurity. Never give a straight answer. When asked, "What should I do about my philandering husband?" say, "The moon is full only once every twenty-nine days."

BE SILENT

When in doubt, say nothing. And be in doubt most of the time. When asked a question like, "What is the meaning of life?" just smile knowingly but say nothing.

DRESS THE PART

Buy clothes from small, dark shops that smell like Jerry Garcia's dog. Buy the latest fashions from third-world countries like Bangladesh, Sri Lanka, and Canada. Choose weird natural fibers such as hemp and bamboo. Tell people, "You are what you wear."

SURROUND YOURSELF WITH WISE PROPS

Get a staff with feathers and bells on it, plus some Buddha statues, incense burners, and a couple of those winged mermaids from India that you hang from the ceiling like spiritual fighter-plane models.

PLAY WORLD MUSIC

Choose pieces that are all rhythm and no melody. Look up into space once in a while and remark: "Wow, the tabla is playing seven against thirteen."

SMUDGE

Pick some sage or pine needles or poison oak and carry it with you everywhere to purify your surroundings. Set the stuff on fire, then blow it out so that it smolders and drips sparks on the carpet. Use it to stink up your house, meditation studio, hotel room, and rental car.

FAKE A DISABILITY

Many real gurus have physical or developmental limitations that serve as a doorway into the ineffable. Affect a limp, a stammer, or an appreciation of the music of Yanni. Carry a carved and painted cane.

DISCOVER YOUR TOTEM ANIMAL

This is an animal with which you have a spiritual affinity and from whom you draw your power. Choose a totem animal you admire, one whose characteristics you would like to make your own. Mine is the gopher.

Once you have become a wise elder, you can bask in the unconditional love and respect of lesser beings and fill your plate first at crowded potluck suppers.

PART 4

Families

34. Husbands R Us

There are more old women than old men because women live longer. Lots of single older women would like to hook up with a nice single man, but the pickings are slim. The single older men who are available are usually available for a reason, like they just got out of rehab, their ex wife is buried in the cellar, or they line their hat with tinfoil so Bill Gates can't read their thoughts.

The more tolerable men are usually taken already by women who like them well enough but wish they'd get out of the house for a few hours and stop hovering. Thousands of serviceable husbands suffer low self-esteem because they are underfoot and therefore underappreciated at home.

To address both the older-dude shortage and underfootness, I have launched Husbands R Us, a nonprofit agency that loans older, well-maintained husbands to women who could use one for a spell. Here's how it works:

Wives with underfoot husbands sign them up for four two-hour sessions a week. We've found that two hours is as long as the average husband can successfully feign sociability. For the wife, two hours of blessed solitude is enough time to watch a chick flick, make a phone call, or pound down a couple of highballs and straighten out. For the single woman, two hours is long enough to get some pictures hung, move some heavy furniture, chat with the borrowed husband, and come to the realization that being single the other 166 hours of the week is not necessarily a bad thing.

Husbands R Us is not a dating service enabling adultery. In fact, we're the opposite. The husbands and the interested single women fill out a comprehensive profiling questionnaire designed to pair them up according to subtle psychological and demographic parameters. This is the genius part. We use reverse dating-service software that guarantees that the loaner husbands and single women will be totally incompatible. This way, husbands are glad to get out of the house and spend time with a woman who purports to want them, but they are even gladder to leave after two hours and go back to their wives.

If this catches on, I hope to franchise a for-profit version. Imagine the improvements in geriatric mental health. All women over sixty-five could have 5 percent of a husband, about as much as a woman really needs. Wives could have a few hours to put their feet up and detox from an overdose of hubby. Husbands could have a woman on the side whom they see a couple of times a week but don't share a joint bank account with—what all men fantasize about, anyway. I see nothing but upside here, a win-win-win situation.

35. Why Women Live Longer

One of my retirement projects is figuring out why women live longer than men. I've made a study of the subject, spending as much time with women as I can, observing them closely. It was easy to infiltrate their ranks. Men would never be so lax about security. Most of my men friends are still working, so they're too busy to just hang out and are suspicious of your motives if you suggest going out for a drink or a cup of coffee for no reason. But women, even busy women who have full-time jobs, are more willing to drop everything and go out for a cup of coffee, especially if it involves espresso and biscotti.

Women go to great lengths to appear normal, but I'm sure there is some kind of conspiracy going on, some great secret to their longevity that they take pains to disguise. Please consider: women spend an incredible amount of time with other women. They *must* be up to something. They meet for breakfast and talk about their plans for the day over a Danish and a latte. They stop by midmorning for a cappuccino and biscotti and talk about what they're wearing. At lunch they talk about their kids. They schedule their afternoon coffee breaks together to talk about husbands and boyfriends and continue the conversation at happy hour after work. Women go out to dinner and talk about what to get Betty for her birthday and how they fell off the diet that day, what with all the Danish and lattes and biscotti and cappuccinos.

The upshot of this incessant meeting and dining and coffee klatching is that women are in great demand. Even women with weak social skills are pulled into circles of other women who are thirsty for their company. According to my friend Mabel, this socializing means that women get more human contact, more hugs, more information about and involvement in the lives of others, and that's why they live longer. Mabel says that most men come late to the party. We think we're too busy for connection, when really we're just asocial. When busy, asocial men eventually retire; they're too far behind the social power-curve. They can't break into the social sphere, so they die of loneliness, which is basically lack of attention, lack of that subtle but necessary message: "Oh, I see you're still alive."

I don't buy Mabel's theory because careful observation shows that women don't always hug. They don't always tell stories about their children or husbands or boyfriends. They don't always meet in the same place. I've eliminated countless variables and have come to the conclusion that Mabel's "human contact" theory is just a smokescreen to hide the real reason women live longer than men.

For a long time I thought it was the Danish or the biscotti. Then I realized the truth is even more basic than that: it's the coffee.

36. The Geographical Fix

After trying every economy, you may still not be able to make it where you're living now. You may have to move somewhere cheaper, where the cost of living is lower, and your fixed income will go farther. Historically, this was California, then Florida, then Arizona, then Costa Rica, then Mexico. Now the only true bargains remaining are the slums of Calcutta, the caves of Afghanistan, and suburban Darfur.

But that kind of thinking is pessimistic, typical of those who think the U-Haul trailer is half empty. Let's assume it's half full and be logical and organized about finding a place to retire. Visit towns you like. Spend an hour walking around the neighborhoods, chatting with people, browsing the stores. Cross a town off your list if you get mugged, bitten by an alligator, or arrested for vagrancy. Stop by the local chamber of commerce and quiz the volunteer behind the counter. You'll find this person a fund of useful information, since she, herself, retired there two years ago and bought the last bargain home in town.

Go online and Google "best places to retire." I just did, and *Money* magazine's site says the current utopias are Prescott, Arizona (too hot for me); Holland, Michigan (too much snow); Walla Walla, Washington (too many Ws); St. Simon's Island, Georgia (an island!?); and Williamsburg, Virginia (too many Civil War re-enactments). My strongest objection to these towns is that they became too crowded and expensive ten minutes after they went up on the website. You might as well throw darts at a map, like the editors of *Money* magazine do.

I came up with this handy checklist to help me find the best retirement spot:

- ☐ Close enough to my favorite friends and relatives
- ☐ Far enough from the difficult friends and relatives
- ☐ Affordable (Dirt cheap)
- ☐ Sound economy (Streets paved with gold)
- ☐ Lots of nice houses to choose from
- ☐ Pleasant climate
- ☐ Near recreation I enjoy (Foosball, quoits, helicopter skiing)
- ☐ Safe
- ☐ Culturally rich (Opera and Baskin-Robbins)
- ☐ Good medical care nearby
- ☐ Friendly people
- ☐ Beautiful scenery

If you know someplace that meets all these criteria, please let me know.

Actually, no place is perfect, and no place is attractive to everyone. Plus, moving won't solve all your problems. In Alcoholics Anonymous, they say the "geographical fix" never works because wherever drunks move, they're still drunks. Likewise, wherever you move, you'll still be an older, retired person on a fixed income. As Yoda, Mr. Natural, and Alan Watts said, wherever you go, there you are. That's good news if you like yourself. If you don't, you can't run far or fast enough to escape, so you might as well stay where you are and work on your self-esteem. May I suggest *Self-Esteem*, a classic self-help book by Patrick Fanning and Matthew McKay?

37. The Nation of Two

In Kurt Vonnegut's early novel, *Mother Night*, the hero and heroine refer to themselves as a "nation of two," meaning that their allegiance is to each other, not to America or Germany or any of the other warring parties in the second World War. In retirement, many couples form a nation of two. It's an effective way of closing ranks, watching each other's back, combining strengths, and compensating for weaknesses.

You and your partner may have had serious border skirmishes in the past, but you have to transcend that now. Consider the hurts and slights, the neglect and betrayal, the affairs and trial separations—all of your historical baggage—to be the birth pangs, the inevitable working-out of the dialectic of your glorious nation of two. In other words, get over it. Grow up. Realize that at your age and in your situation, no one else would have you, so you're stuck with each other.

Repeat to each other this comforting cliché: "What doesn't kill you makes you stronger." Even if you suspect that what doesn't kill you makes you seriously wounded. Declare a cease-fire. Sign a nonaggression pact. Form an alliance with your partner. Find ways that the two of you, however compromised by age and infirmity, can add up to one fully functional person:

I'll be your eyes, you be my ears.

I'll be your legs, you be my memory.

I'll be your bookkeeper, you be my heart.

I'll be your spinach, you be my sunshine.

As you can see, this can get goofy after a while. Be careful that your nation of two doesn't go off the deep end. You don't want to become a rogue state like North Korea or Libya, pursuing your own cuckoo agenda, making your own nukes out of cardboard and tinfoil while your citizens starve. If it begins to seem like the whole world is out of step with you, dissolve your government and hold new elections.

My friend Jack Johnson was basically conservative, and his wife, Bernice, was pretty liberal. But in retirement, they formed a bipartisan coalition combining the worst of both camps. "I'm red, she's blue," Jack explained. "But we work together to dominate the whole neighborhood. Our sphere of influence extends in a 'Pax Johnsoniana' all the way to Webster Street. The homeowners association got up a resolution censoring us, but screw 'em. It's our destiny and sacred responsibility to police this subdivision. Last week we invaded the Harts' on the pretext of playing bridge, started a grease fire in the kitchen as a diversion, and made off with their Cuisinart, six Hummel figures, and a leaf blower."

Since hitting on this metaphor for retired family life, international affairs have ceased to depress me. Instead, every new revolution, famine, and assassination gives me new insight on how to survive and prosper in my home.

38. Retired Relationships

When you retire, your relationship with your spouse can change profoundly. Many couples have to get to know each other all over again. It can feel like dating a stranger, but without the complications of immaturity, inexperience, or physical attraction.

For one thing, you and your spouse will need to renegotiate the division of labor in daily life. For instance, my Uncle Sampson retired from a job in aerospace, and his wife, Nadine, stopped doing dishes and weeding the garden. Sam had more time for his hobby of building rocket models, and Nadine had more time for her part-time business making and selling potholders with holiday themes. They puttered along, companionably side-by-side, modeling and sewing while the dishes piled up and the weeds took over the garden. Finally, Nadine had to insist that Sam pitch in with the dishes and weeding. Sam put down his model Saturn booster, looked around at the mess, realized the changed nature of his relationship with Nadine, and went back to work as a consultant.

Your values change when you retire. Things that used to seem important are now nothing to you, and things you never thought about before are suddenly crucial to your happiness. My Aunt Dolores never gave the TV schedule a thought when she was working, but upon retirement, she was in constant competition with Uncle Roscoe for possession of the remote. Their marriage was barely saved in the eleventh hour by TiVo and Roscoe's macular degeneration.

When I retired, I suddenly became the cheap one in my marriage. I started acting like my grandpa in the Great

Depression, mashing slivers of hand soap into "new" balls of soap and using pliers to squeeze out the last of the toothpaste. Nancy had to shock me out of it by filling my Christmas stocking with Crest and Dial.

When your partner retires, you may have to help him or her cope with depression. Upon retirement, my Uncle Griff fell into a pit of meaninglessness—plus the Red Sox fell into a horrible slump. Aunt Shirrelle encouraged him to get more exercise by putting his socks and underwear in different drawers. She exposed him to more sunlight by flashing a mirror in his eyes to wake him up every morning. She took his mind off the Red Sox by rubbing his feet while watching hockey on TV with him. It was the feet that finally did it. Griff was so ticklish that he had to get up and take a walk to get away from her. Walks in the open air cheered him up and the crisis was passed.

39. Grandchildren: Your New Playmates

The average young couple is not prepared for parenthood. They don't have enough experience, education, maturity, money, or time. After all, it wasn't that long ago that they were kids themselves, smoking dope behind the 7-Eleven, tattooing themselves with ballpoint pens, and espousing such practical philosophies as, "Who needs a car when you have a skateboard?"

That's why nature evolved grandparents—as a safety net for grandchildren. Grandparents know all about childrearing, having raised what they consider to be the better half of the average young couple. Grandparents usually have plenty of money and positively reek of maturity. *Retired* grandparents are even better, since they have nothing but time to devote to their grandkids.

Now, some grandparents brag that they get to play with their grandkids, spoil them rotten, enjoy them until everybody is tired and cranky, then skip off home and leave the average young couple to deal with the whiney fallout of their meddling. This is just a smoke screen. The "playing" and "spoiling" perfected by grandparents are cleverly disguised lessons in Real Life 101.

If you're new at the grandparent game, here are a few guidelines to get you started:

BE A POSITIVE ROLE MODEL

If you get lost driving a grandchild to the park, say, "I'm *positive* it was around here somewhere." Grandchildren can be very observant and critical. Even when they point out your mistakes, stay positive and never admit that you are wrong.

BE CONSISTENT

In real life, people often disappoint and seldom change. Prepare your grandchildren for this by always doing the same things the same way, whether they like it or not. Refuse to cut the crust off the sandwich; take them to the pony ride that terrifies them and the doll museum that bores them. Be a consistent factor in their lives, something they can count on.

REINFORCE GOOD BEHAVIOR

Kids respond best to positive reinforcement. For instance, they need the courage to ask for what they want in life. So, whatever your grandchild asks for, give it freely: cookies, ice cream, video games, ponies, trips to Disney World—refuse them nothing. You are building their character, buttressing their personal power, and reinforcing their sense of entitlement.

DISCOURAGE BAD BEHAVIOR

When your grandchild behaves badly—fussing, crying, saying "no," pooping diapers, messing with your stuff, or otherwise bothering you—you must punish this evil. But don't call it that. We don't punish evil these days. We negatively reinforce undesirable behavior by levying natural consequences: when your precious descendant bugs you, send it back to the average young couple.

40. While We're at It

Our friends Steve and Sarah are members of the Sandwich Generation. They had their son, Charlie, late in life and kicked him out of the house just in time for Steve's father to move in. Grandpa was grateful for the opportunity to live with them, but he wasn't too crazy about the heavy-metal decor Charlie left behind in his old room. The two-by-four and plywood loft bed, eight feet off the floor, was also problematic.

Steve had just retired and had some free time. Like many retirees, he thought remodeling the house would be a good way to kick-start their new lifestyle. His first impulse was to demolish the loft bed, scrape the fluorescent skull stickers off the ceiling, patch the fist-sized holes in the purple walls, and slap on a coat of white paint.

Then he uttered the fateful four words: "While we're at it ..."

"While we're at it," he asked Sarah, "why don't we add on to the front of the house, pushing it out to the edge of the deck?"

"Perfect," she said. "Then we could knock out the wall between the living room and Charlie's old room and turn that space into an L-shaped music alcove. It would be great for parties."

"That would make the guest room big enough for Dad, and we could get a grand piano."

"And I could leave my music stands and instruments set up all the time."

"While we're at it, we could update the guest bathroom."

"How about a cathedral ceiling?" Sarah suggested.

"With skylights," Steve chimed in.

"Wainscoting!" they shouted together.

Two busy years later, the plans were drawn, permits were pulled, and they were ready to break ground. But first they took one weekend off to clear out Charlie's old room, patch the larger holes, scrape off the skull stickers, and paint the loft platform so that Dad could finally move in.

Three hectic years later, the whole front half of the house was raw concrete, studs, and plastic sheeting. Dad was living in Steve and Sarah's room, they were in a trailer in the driveway, and the kitchen was full of couches and music stands and the TV.

In another two years, the remodel was finally done, and it was beautiful. Steve had gone back to work full-time to pay for it all. Sarah was working half-time and was too busy to play music. Dad had moved to a nursing home where they were better equipped to care for him. Their son, Charlie, had lost his job and had gone through a messy divorce, so he moved back home, into the gorgeous new guest room.

There's no particular moral to this story. It's just life—what happens while we're at it.

PART 5

Your Body

41. Join a Gym

As someone with the muscle tone, flexibility, and range of motion of a hat rack, I'm in favor of retired people joining a gym. But make sure it's the right gym.

In my town, the young gym is owned by a local TV personality, a starlet with buns, abs, and hair of steel. It's on a busy street and has big windows, bright lights, lots of mirrors, rock music, and shiny chrome exercise machines that look like futuristic motorcycles. It's full of sweaty twenty-something contortionists in spandex who go there to see and be seen. They sing along with their iPods, chew gum in time to the elliptical striders, and grunt explosively every time they lift a weight.

I go to the oldster gym that is owned by a chiropractor and his wife. She's a fifty-five-year-old ballet dancer who paid him a fortune for adjustments before they were married, until she realized it would be cheaper to buy the cow. Their gym has small windows on a quiet street, dim lighting, and so few mirrors that vampires could work out there. It's decorated in a Greco-Roman style that went out with Sophocles. They play restful classical music, and the exercise machines are older models in white enamel and stainless steel, like hospital equipment. The members wear sensible, form-concealing sweats and move slowly and carefully. It's considered gauche to grunt or break a sweat.

The young gym is all about getting better: building bigger muscles, increasing endurance, improving flexibility. Folks there pound down energy drinks, chatter about sports, and jump around in cardio kickboxing class like hyperactive kangaroos.

Once in a while they pull a muscle or break a finger playing hockey or basketball.

The oldster gym is all about staying the same: retaining some muscle tone, maintaining flexibility, preserving range of motion. What we do is more like physical therapy than exercise. We sip exotic waters, complain about our joints, and shuffle through Jazzercise class like the zombies in *Night of the Living Dead*. Once in a while somebody breaks a hip reaching for the soap in the locker room.

Look around when you're gym shopping. If you see any sweat or belly buttons, leave immediately. If people are talking about "reps" and "spotting" the lifter, that's a bad sign. If the person at the front counter comes on like a peppy coach, you are probably in the wrong gym. You want the place with the gray sweatshirts, where people are talking about their arthritis and how the stair stepper makes them pee. The class listing should contain words like "gentle" and "low impact." If the person who greets you has the demeanor of a good funeral director and asks you if there is any heart disease in your family, you have found the right gym.

42. Taking a Walk

"Taking a walk" sounds so simple, but it's not. When we were young, my wife and I would take a walk in a state park, see an interesting trail marker, and say, "Let's do it." Two hours later we'd return to where we started and continue our walk, unwinded, mildly diverted and amused by our seven- or eight-mile detour.

These days, it's different. A walk in our local city park requires more planning than a landing on Mars. First we have to pack the geezer survival kits: two ergonomic day packs filled to bursting with prescription medications, allergy pills, three brands of anti-inflammatories, eyedrops, sunscreen, ACE bandages, TUMS, Handi Wipes, "His 'n' Hers" blood-pressure cuffs, a Sterno camp stove, ginseng tea bags, baseball caps with neck shades, rain ponchos, a bird book, tree book, mammal book, reptile book, and invertebrate book, binoculars, monocular, microscope, dissection kit, water-purification tablets, flare gun, snakebite kit, moleskin, bandages, waterproof matches, hot and cold sprain wraps, vitaminized artesian spring water from Sri Lanka—the list goes on way longer than I feel like writing or you'd want to read, if you even got *this* far.

If we think about it, we throw in some carrot sticks or chopped egg-white sandwiches on high-fiber bread. Then we have to check the weather, download maps to the GPS unit, charge our cell phones, and waterproof our new hiking boots with the computer-designed orthopedic inserts. You'd think we were trekking through the Himalayas in a blizzard instead of strolling around the bird-watching loop on a sunny day. After all this, we dawdle around the loop for half a mile and return to the car, exhausted and sore for the next three days.

To avoid all of this rigmarole, many retirees take up mall hiking. Malls have smooth, level surfaces, no weather, benches to rest on, and security guards instead of snakes and mountain lions. When you need a bird book, go to Barnes & Noble. When you need a cappuccino, drop into Starbucks. When you're tired, just stop for some vitaminized artesian spring water or defibrillation.

The design of malls is changing in areas with lots of retirees. You're starting to see trail markers, scenic overlooks, and "No wading" signs on fountains. Older malls are renting out pushcarts in the middle of the aisles to intercept the walkers who never enter the actual stores. They sell things walkers need like jewelry, perfume, and framed prints of dogs playing poker.

My wife and I tried mall hiking once, but old habits die hard. They didn't like it in Banana Republic when I fired up the Sterno cooker to brew some ginseng tea.

43. Life in the Slow Lane

I love my doctor, but I suspect he may be a frustrated English major because he loves to use similes when talking about my health. Like the other day, when I went to see him about my sore hip, he told me that bodies are like used cars: as they age, parts wear out, and they need more frequent maintenance.

"In that case," I said, "I'd like to trade my car in on a new model."

"No," he explained. "You don't *have* the car—you *are* the car. You have to keep yourself on the road as long as possible."

"So the arthritis in my hip is like a bad wheel bearing?"

"Right. You have to baby it and make it last till you're old enough for a hip replacement."

"Maybe I should put myself up on blocks for a few years."

"Just drive in the slow lane."

I hate driving in the slow lane. It means I should stop playing volleyball because it's too hard on the hip. But volleyball has deep emotional significance to me. I met my wife playing volleyball. In the summer, we play every Wednesday evening. It's a tradition, one of the pivots around which our community of friends revolves. But my doctor was correct: it's hard on the hip.

So I cut back to two games of volleyball each Wednesday. And I don't dive for the low balls anymore. I let my son do that. Eventually I'll be sitting on the sidelines, hitting the ball when it comes out of bounds in my direction. But we'll still host the game, even when the players are all my son's generation, and we old hulks are sitting up on blocks on the sidelines, criticizing the quality of play, which was much higher when we were late models in the fast lane.

Life in the slow lane means that I probably will never be on the Olympic volleyball team, that volleyball-wise, I somehow got over the hill without ever getting to the top.

On the other hand, life in the slow lane means I can take the blue-line highway through life. I can track down the perfect roadhouse barbecue. I can pull over for a nap or a chat with old friends. I can stop and smell the roses, if I still have a sense of smell and give a damn about roses.

Frankly, when I get those new wheel bearings, I'm going for one last spin in the fast lane.

44. Yoga Is Better than Glucosamine

As a kid, I loved to find lucky pennies on the ground. After age fifty, I started doing a cost/benefit analysis, and my current policy is no bending over for anything less than a five-dollar bill.

At fifty-eight, I started taking glucosamine, MSM, omega 3-6-9, shark cartilage, multivitamins, gummi bears—whatever the Internet told me to take for joint pain. I kept forgetting to take the pills at meals, when I was supposed to take them. I'd suddenly remember at bedtime and have to take the pills with a late-night bowl of cereal and a cup of hot chocolate. So that was working out all right, but my joints still hurt after six months of nutritional supplements. The extra weight from the cereal and cocoa might have been a contributing factor.

So, I enrolled in a weekly yoga class. At first I couldn't sit in the full-lotus or the half-lotus position but had to devise what I call the "half-assed" position. I felt like a wooden mannequin in a roomful of real people. A slim young woman named Lani was next to me. She could sit in full-lotus, bend forward, and fold herself up like a deck chair. My "sit up straight" and "bend forward" were indistinguishable. I could fold myself up as easily as folding a stainless-steel barstool.

But the class was pleasant, somewhat interesting, and I was feeling mildly self-satisfied for sticking with it. Then, one evening I was walking across the Office Depot parking lot. Suddenly a cymbal crashed, a tight spotlight hit me, a ninety-piece orchestra struck up a stirring tune, and I tap-danced into the store singing "Gotta Dance!"

No, actually, it just felt like that. What really happened was that I noticed I was walking upright, with good posture and a spring in my step, whistling "Somewhere Over the Rainbow" under my breath. I nearly stumbled when I realized: *Nothing hurts. I feel … what's the word? Fine. The yoga must be working.*

The original purpose of yoga was to prepare for meditation, to render the body "weightless" or "invisible" so that your mind is free from the distraction of bodily sensations. In front of Office Depot, I experienced a moment of weightlessness, a moment when all my usual aches and pains, restrictions and compensations, had become invisible. My mind was free to float into a mental musical-comedy moment, which is about as close to meditation as I'm likely to get.

I keep coming back to yoga for these "invisible" moments, which happen maybe six times a year. The rest of the time, I make do with the more mundane pleasures of yoga. Every time Lani folds forward I get a glimpse of the butterfly tattoo on her lower back, and I've always loved entomology.

45. Keeping Romance Alive

In your retirement years, you don't have to retire from romance, but sometimes it needs a little help. Life support for your romantic life requires conscious effort, imagination, and planning. For example, Nancy and I make a point of going out for a romantic, candlelit dinner once a week. She goes on Tuesday, and I go on Friday.

Seriously, it's important to spend quality time together, and it's hard when everyone's so busy. Nancy and I often reconnect with each other through our book club. We both love to read, but reading is an inherently private experience. By belonging to a book club, we are exposed to some of the same titles and get to share part of our intellectual lives that we might otherwise tend to keep to ourselves. The book-club meeting is one time each month when we know we'll be in the same place, at the same time, talking about the same thing: why we were too busy to read the book.

The language of love changes a little in retirement. I notice that we don't surprise each other with little gestures anymore: the single perfect rose; the chocolate truffle on the pillow; the smiley faces and little hearts on the shopping list. But that's okay. We have other ways of showing we care. These days, if I remember to buy coffee filters, that's love. If they're the brown, recycled kind, that's devotion. If they are actually the right size for the coffee machine, that's as good as a dozen orchids and a string quartet.

I do know one genuinely romantic older couple. My Uncle Randy and Aunt Cherie recently celebrated their thirtieth wedding anniversary. They are on a budget, so they went to McDonald's. But they made it romantic. Randy brought his own wine and an ice bucket. Cherie brought cloth napkins, one perfect rose in a bud vase, and her grandma's real silver flatware, polished to a high shine. They each had a different Neil Young song playing on their iPod, humming along out of sync, kind of loud because they're both deaf, and you can't use the iPod and the hearing aid at the same time. So, they're kissing and bellowing at each other, calling each other "Big Mac" and "Cherie Pie."

Sure it's silly, maybe even creepy, but they didn't get embarrassed. They didn't even get thrown out—not until Randy started drinking cold duck out of her orthopedic cross-trainer. And everything turned out fine. The lawsuit was dropped, and their agent is pitching some TV-commercial ideas to McDonald's and iPod.

46. Sex

Most things in nature are subtle, but not the sex drive. Peacocks have their huge tails and moose have their antlers. Humans used to have codpieces and miniskirts. In recent history, humans have become more subtle about sex, probably due to our aging population. For example, in high school I remember that sex even accounted for how we walked. Guys swaggered as if their equipment were so huge they could hardly swing a leg around it, while girls minced along as if their privates were so deep they might split in half like a pistachio shell. Now those same folks walk identically—as if they were carrying a moose on their shoulders and each step costs them a dollar.

I took a walk in our local high-school campus recently to see if young people still walk like we did when we were in their shoes. After I posted bond and security released me, I noticed much gender confusion. Most guys couldn't swagger because their low-riding pants would fall down. The girls who were mincing were holding hands with other girls who weren't. In several cases, I couldn't identify the gender at all. Nevertheless, there was a lot of snoogling and kissing going on, so I came away reassured that young people may dress and walk funny, but they are still definitely interested in sex, which is a good thing. If it were up to me, we'd be extinct by now.

Actually, I'm not disinterested in sex. I'm interested in sex the same way I'm interested in space travel and black holes. I'm fascinated, but I'll probably never go there. I think most people are like that about sex. It occupies a lot of our imagination but takes up very little of our time. We're like rats conditioned to constantly push a button that only once in a great while actually delivers a food pellet. They say that men think about sex something like six times a minute. We're the prize rats. We're pushing that doorbell all the time, but only one time in a million do we get a ding-dong. If we could harness that energy for something constructive, we'd have Wal-Marts on Mars by now. Well, maybe we're better off not harnessing that energy.

Sexual behavior is hard to change. Psychologists have found that people often change by pretending to be the way they want to be. For example, a shy person can pretend to be outgoing, and eventually they really become more outgoing. The same process does not apply across the board in sex. A newly married man can pretend not to be interested in other women, and seventy or eighty years later, it's somewhat true. However, a newly married woman can pretend to be sexy, but at the end of the same period of time, it's mostly false. This deserves more research.

47. Intimate Communication

One of the few consolations of aging is that you are finally mature enough to talk frankly and without embarrassment about sex.

Right.

Inside, we are all sexually sixteen years old. Still embarrassed by sex, still obsessed with sex, way beyond the age at which it's attractive to do anything about it. Even when I'm 104 years old, being wheeled into the hospital for my fourth round of Peruvian horn toad stem-cell treatments, if I spot some beautiful, young candy striper at the front desk, I'll suck in my stomach. I'll square my shoulders and attempt to send that instinctive, mammalian message: "Please let me father your children."

The gung-ho sex manuals of the seventies encouraged older couples to tell each other what still turns them on, what they still like to do, and what doesn't interest them anymore. They counseled women to take the initiative instead of waiting to be asked. They told older men to take risks and start something, even when afraid of rejection or worried that we won't be able to finish what we started.

That's all wrong. In the twenty-first century, intimate communication between older partners needs to be more subtle and indirect, a matter of exquisitely sensitive hints. For example, at my house, it's important to my wife, Nancy, that we reconnect physically during the holidays. Last December twenty-fifth, I dumped out my Christmas stocking and found a little bottle of personal lubricant in among the candy canes, tangerines, and bars of soap. I'm good at picking up subtle clues like this, so we did manage to reconnect once last year. However, in terms of male recovery time, it's really too bad that New Year's Eve comes so soon after Christmas.

Talking frankly about sex is risky. Although it's no secret that a man's libido diminishes with age, it would be foolhardy honesty for a woman to say to her husband, "Your fire doesn't burn as brightly as it used to." He might reply with equal frankness, "That's because your flue don't draw as good as it used to."

As we have grown older together, Nancy and I have developed our own subtle and nuanced way of talking about our sexual desires. It's gotten so that we can't even hear certain words in their normal meaning. The other day my dentist said his dog gets very frisky whenever he mentions treats, and I started blushing furiously.

48. Grooming

You see them outside restaurants in Scottsdale, Miami, Phoenix, Seattle—in retirement-friendly cities across the nation. They appear around 6:30 p.m., when the early-bird specials expire: flocks of seniors who prove beyond a doubt that retirement brings with it a grooming crisis of biblical proportions.

When you retire, you are no longer subject to any kind of dress code, but with this new freedom comes responsibility. Your appearance can run downhill fast, especially if you move to a different climate or to a city where you don't know any barbers or hairdressers and where you have no history of sartorial restraint.

Twenty-somethings can look gorgeous in ragged cutoffs, messy hair, and dirty T-shirts. You can't. Somewhere past middle age, everyone comes to an evolutionary fork in the road. The wide, smooth path leads comfortably downhill. If you take it, you will devolve slowly into a dowdy, seedy, weird-looking oldster. The road less traveled is rocky and steep, but taking it means that you may evolve into the kind of clean, elegant gent or lady who is referred to as "well preserved." Both roads end up in the same place, but the road-less-traveled folks will have something nice to wear to their funerals.

When I first retired, I regressed to the jeans, T-shirt, and beard that I wore in my twenties. Then Nancy gave me the bad news that I no longer looked like James Dean playing Hamlet. She said I looked more like Tim Allen playing Santa Claus. So I shaved the beard and got a forty-dollar haircut from a stylist in a salon instead of a semiannual buzz cut from Nancy in the kitchen. Our fashion-conscious friend, Linda, took me to a men's boutique where I bought three silk shirts and two pair of silk pants for more than six hundred dollars. It took over four hours, and the whole wardrobe would fit in the back pocket of my jeans. I'm not allowed to paint or work on cars in these flimsy clothes. But at least I don't look like Santa Claus anymore. With my new hairdo, I look more like a cross between Pee-wee Herman and Margaret Thatcher.

Linda helped me prepare this short course in retired fashion and grooming:

MEN

DON'T wear white shoes or belts, sandals with socks, or stubble. All shorts and color combos must be vetted by a woman.

DO trim all hair, beards, mustaches, etc. This includes nose hairs, eyebrows, ears, and wherever else your Wolfman genes are expressed.

WOMEN

DON'T wear swoopy eyeglasses, heavy makeup, lilac scents, small dotty prints, blue hair, outfits that hit dead center at the waist, or orthopedic anything.

DO get your colors done (I have no idea what this means) and wear clothes that *fit*—rather than concealing extra weight, baggy outfits actually make you look fatter.

49. Aging Gracefully

I wish "gracefully" in the title meant that we can all have a graceful old body, but that's not my point. Although some retirees stay fit and attractive, I find that the older I get, the more draconian the laws of physics become. Gravity increases, inertia is harder to overcome, and my body mysteriously acquires more mass. Everything sags, bulges, wrinkles, collapses, leaks, or malfunctions. I limp creakily from day to day in a manner most ungraceful.

Here, "graceful" refers to attitude—the way you think and talk about aging. At some point, you stop complaining about your age and start bragging about it. To use my favorite old-car metaphor, you stop turning back your odometer and forget about the new paint job. You let everyone see what they already know anyway—that you are not a new Acura. You're a 1950 Willys that has traveled a lot miles, some of them on unpaved dirt roads.

It helps to find a role model. Google "famous people born in _____ (your birth year)." Finding out that you share a birth year with Jimmy Carter or Meryl Streep can give you some reflected glory. Try to find celebs who are still alive and vigorous. I'm proud to say that Lyle Littlecroft, the inventor of a sewing-machine attachment for whipstitching nylon, was born the same year as I and is still alive and dynamically managing his Buttons 'n' Notions shop in Lincoln, Nebraska.

The only thing worse than being old is being young. Being young is beautiful, but being old is comfortable. Try this exercise: Go to a high-school or college campus. Pick out the most attractive, healthy, smart-looking young person you see, and pick one of these scenarios:

1. You can be turned into that kid, with his or her childhood, family, memories, personality, talents, etc.

2. You can be transported into that kid's body, with all your personality and memories intact, but in the kid's situation—being a minor, at the mercy of parents and teachers, no money, etc.

3. You can be transported into that kid's body, but you remain who you are, where you are, with all your relationships and assets intact.

Nobody picks number one, because it's indistinguishable from death—without your memories and personality, you are not you anymore. You're a goner. Very few people pick number two, because who wants to fight through the painful passages of youth again? Almost everybody picks number three—they just want the body of youth, not the limits and uncertainties of youth. We treasure our experience, however traumatic, because it's what makes us uniquely ourselves.

50. Life as an Old Car

I often think of my body as an old car that will run longer
if I take good care of it. It requires good driving habits, such
as moderate exercise, periodic maintenance like teeth cleaning, and occasional major repairs in the form of surgery. You
have to wash it, fuel it, stop it from smoking, check the tire/
blood pressure, and adjust things with haircuts and visits to the
chiropractor.

Movie stars have exceptionally nice bodies, like Ferraris.
Other people are more handsome or coordinated than average,
the equivalent of Mercedes. Some long-lived people come from
Toyota stock. Bodybuilders are like Hummers. Sickly people are
like Jaguars. Most of us have Ford and Chevy genes.

Like a car, a body slowly wears out and needs more attention as it ages. Some places spring leaks and other places dry up.
Headlights and sight dim and have to be upgraded with halogen
and eyeglasses. Ears and car stereos weaken and must be renewed
with hearing aids and new speakers. The heater and passions
cool. You start smelling like old dog and motor oil. Eventually,
you will probably need new ball joints and a hip replacement.
And no matter how well you take care of it, a body looks and
performs worse with time. Even with a personal trainer and a
face-lift—the bodily equivalents of detailing and a repaint—you
are never really as good as new.

My old philosophy professor would say that by treating my
body like an object, separate from my "real" self, I am guilty of
Cartesian mind/body dualism, an error of thinking that leads
to alienation. I say phooey to that; it's only a useful metaphor.

By seeing myself as a junker that I'm trying to keep on the road, I get a little distance from my bodily woes. Bodily maintenance becomes a daily spiritual practice, like polishing a classic roadster.

On the other hand, life as an old car is not for everyone. My cousin Harry is a mechanical illiterate who has never opened the hood of any car he has ever owned. To him, oil changes are mysterious rites carried out at the dealership by priestly technicians. The old-car metaphor is not only useless to him—it could be harmful. If he could be convinced that his body was really an old car, he would immediately want to trade it in, as he does his real cars when the ashtrays get full of gum wrappers.

Come to think of it, maybe we do trade in. Maybe reincarnation is an accurate description of how old minds get hooked up to new bodies. In that case, I want to come back as a hydrogen fuel-cell hybrid. Red, please.

PART 6

Spirituality

51. The Doldrums

One morning in early retirement, I looked around the living room and everything seemed dull and dim, as if somebody had replaced all the 100-watt light bulbs with compact fluorescents. I wandered into my office, picked up the manuscript of my great-American-novel-in-progress, and listlessly let it fall back on the desk, all twenty-two pages of it.

"What's the use?" I asked myself.

I drifted out to the barn and contemplated the chassis of my half-restored 1951 MG TD. This is the car in which I learned to drive stick shift at age sixteen. I've been looking forward to restoring one for years.

"So what?" I thought. I went back to bed.

I was in the doldrums. Clinically, these latitudes are known as "situational depression," but I call them the doldrums because it feels like somebody took all the wind out of my sails. I don't feel up to going anywhere, doing anything, or seeing anybody.

After resting up for a couple of days in bed, I mustered enough energy to turn on the TV. Three months later, I turned it off and went out to the barn to work on the MG. Time had cured my depression, as it always does. But it's a lousy cure because it takes too long. And it doesn't last. Three months later, I drifted into the doldrums again, put the wrenches down, and turned the TV back on.

I finally worked out a cure that attacks the symptoms head-on:

1. **Diagnosis.** I tell myself, "You idiot, you're depressed again! Don't worry, it's only a feeling,

and it will pass in time. However, if you'd like to avoid three months of M*A*S*H and *Battlestar Galactica* reruns, proceed to Step Two."

2. **First aid.** I turn a doorknob instead of turning on the TV. I go outside and start walking. Natural outdoor light and physical activity are immediate antidotes to depression. I've never seen a depressed pigeon. When in doubt, I walk to the coffee shop and order a triple-shot café latte. The occasional caffeine overdose energizes me better than SNRIs, MAOIs, or Saint-John's-wort.

3. **Treatment.** While I'm sitting in the coffee shop, I call someone and make a plan to do something together. Going to the movies with a friend is better than watching TV, because it gets you out of the house and involves some human contact. Dinner out is better, because you can talk. Helping somebody remodel their bathroom or prune their trees is best, because the activity is inherently interesting to me and I can talk about the task itself as well as about how depressed I am.

52. Maintaining Human Contact

One night in my men's group, we were talking about superheroes. The group has been meeting twice a month for over fifteen years, so we've exhausted all of the good topics. I posed the question, "Would you rather be able to fly or be invisible?"

"No question," George replied. "I'd fly—I've been invisible for years."

George has found retirement a very lonely time because he can no longer depend on his job as an IRS tax auditor to supply social interaction. Retired, cut off, and alone, he has no one in his life to complain when he's late, argue with his ridiculous notions, or make him look stupid in meetings. The men's group performs some of these functions, but there is still a huge social void in George's life.

He has tried joining service clubs, but the Rotary made him dizzy, and he's allergic to Elk, Moose, and other ungulates. The local branch of Al Qaeda rejected his application because he listed his religion as Baptist. The only clubs he has stuck with are AAA and the Safeway Club. But they provide very little social interaction, even if you drive a 1972 Dodge Dart and buy your six-packs one can at a time.

George heard that successful retirees make a positive effort every day to converse with a wide variety of people. So, every Monday he goes downtown and accosts passersby, telling them what it was really like at Woodstock, the Betty Ford Clinic, Tralfamadore, and in China with Nixon.

George especially craves physical contact. We end every men's group meeting with a group hug and often have to pry

George's arms off our necks. George has no sense of rhythm, but he goes out folk dancing so he can hold hands with strangers. He tends to stand too close to people in lines. He got in a little trouble at Six Flags last summer when he jumped into the Ball Crawl with the toddlers.

So far, George's best strategy for maintaining human contact has been joining a church that meets in an old warehouse down by the railroad tracks. When he runs out of stories to tell the other church members, he sings a hymn along with the rock band. If he doesn't know the words, he just falls on the floor, writhes around, and speaks in tongues. People crouch down all around him and lay their hands on his body. If he wants even more attention, the preacher can heal him of something. So far he's been healed of blindness, lameness, and leprosy. He is becoming a key member of the congregation.

"Next week they want me to do something with rattlesnakes," George explains. "But heck, it's better than staying home alone."

53. Eccentricity

Do you ever look into the dark night of your soul and think, "I'm really weird"? If so, you are not alone. Everybody thinks that from time to time. People are a lot stranger than people think.

Eccentricity is any unusual behavior for which you can't be put in jail or a straitjacket. Being eccentric just means that you have a unique personality. When you're retired, you have the time and freedom to fully explore and embrace your eccentricity.

For example, I like to sleep outside, under the stars, without a tent. You can get away with that in California, where it almost never rains from June to September. Lying on my back, gazing into the infinite universe, I feel like an insignificant speck of protoplasm infesting the atmospheric scum of a third-rate planet circling a second-rate star, which never fails to cheer me up. Who cares if an insignificant speck has done the dishes or vaccinated his cat?

When I retired, my wife and I started moving our bed out onto the back deck in June. We live on a couple of acres, and our neighbor's house is far away, so this isn't as public as it sounds. We wait all summer for mid-August, when the Perseid meteor showers occur. Most years it's overcast, or we are out of town, sleeping under a ceiling somewhere in August. But last year we went to bed on August 11, not too tired, on a dark, clear night with no moon, and actually saw five shooting stars before we fell asleep. That's about as good as the Perseids get. They really should call it a meteor sprinkle.

Because the Perseid meteor sprinkle is so wimpy, stargazing is also one of the better cures for insomnia. I tell myself that I can't go to sleep until I see a shooting star ... I must keep my eyes open and stay alert ... zzzzzzz.

I just love falling stars. Huckleberry Finn thought that maybe falling stars were rotten and got hove out of the nest, but Jim opined that maybe the moon laid them. Huck thought that might be true since he'd seen a frog lay almost as many. I think about this passage every time I see a falling star. I also have an elaborate fantasy about how you could fake the night sky with lots of black velvet and a gazillion Christmas tree lights.

Although California doesn't have rain in the summer, we do have fog and dew, rather heavy at times. Many mornings, Nancy and I wake up cleaved together like yin and yang—a warm, dry spot surrounded by a damp and dank world of foggy dew. Sometimes we don't get up till nine or ten, after the sun comes out and dries things off. When you're retired, you can do that too.

54. Humor

Some days there's nothing funny about retirement, but you have to laugh anyway. If you don't learn to laugh at trouble as you get older, you'll have nothing to laugh at. It certainly beats complaining. Who would you rather hang out with, someone who laughs all the time or someone who complains all the time? Neither? Well, I get your point.

I should explain how this book came about. The local art center where I volunteer was having Talent Night and they were short of talent. Somebody said, "Pat, you're a writer—write a skit or something." I picked "something" since skits require actors, and all the people who could act were already taken. I did ten minutes of stand-up comedy, people laughed, and I was hooked. I decided that my next book, which was slated to be about retirement, would be humorous in tone. In the course of writing this book, I've come up with some definitive answers to the question, "What's funny?"

FUNNY	NOT FUNNY
Nancy's new hat	My new hat
Sex	Sex
Elected officials	Politics
The unexpected	Surprises

You may have noticed some overlap. That's where it depends on the situation and the audience. Let me explain. One day, when my son was eleven, he put a rubber band around the little lever on the kitchen-sink sprayer, so that when I turned on the water my shirt got soaked. That was *not funny*, and we had a serious talk about how cruel practical jokes are. About a month later, I did it to him, and that was *funny*.

As a retired person, you're probably not interested in doing stand-up comedy or finding out what's funny at my house. You would simply like to be considered an amusing companion rather than a grump. Fortunately, that's simple: instead of complaining, sprinkle your conversation with humor. If you can't think of any actual jokes, that's no problem. A lot of humor involves fuzzy logic and loose, quirky associations that don't really make sense—which comes naturally to retired people.

Just ramble on and occasionally end a sentence with a loud, upward inflection. That's the punch line. Start laughing yourself, and most of your listeners will laugh along with you. Half of them have been trying unsuccessfully to follow you and will laugh because they don't want anyone to think they don't get the joke. The other half have not been paying attention at all, and they'll laugh out of nervous politeness.

To preserve a reputation as a funny person, you only have to say something genuinely funny about one time in ten. The other nine times, you can just be vaguely goofy. And a beneficial side effect of vague goofiness is that you'll be senile six months before anyone notices.

55. Bad Luck

Being from California and in the self-help book business, I've heard and even written things like:

Take responsibility for your own life.

Winners make their own luck.

Visualize what you want, and the universe will manifest it.

These optimistic sayings can make you feel pretty smug if you hit retirement in good health, with plenty of money, and surrounded by loving family and friends. But if you retire sick, broke, and alone, these sayings can really turn on you. They take on a sinister new meaning:

It's your own fault.

You're a loser.

You created a miserable life for yourself.

What straightened me out was being married to Nancy. She's a nurse who has cared for many patients who ate right, exercised, took vitamins, donated to charity, meditated, never smoked or drank—and they got cancer or some other horrible disease anyway.

Nancy says, "You can be as new age and 'human potential' as you like, but bad luck happens. I tell my patients, 'It's not your fault. You're not to blame. You just had bad luck.'"

So I've learned to take the new-age "empowerment" message with a whole cup of salt. Despite all your attempts to control your retirement, life is a gamble and sometimes you're the cooler. There is no cosmic significance to bad luck. Bad luck is no reflection on you or your worth. If the slot machine of your life has come up lemons, tell yourself, "I did my best, day to day, to do what seemed right at the time, and still I had bad luck. It's not anybody's fault, especially mine."

You know that saying, "When life gives you lemons, make lemonade"? That is more new-age b.s. It assumes you can lay your hands on clean water, sugar, ice, a knife, a pitcher—all kinds of additional resources. If you're naked in the Gobi Desert with a lap full of lemons, all you can make is sour sand.

Not that you should expect bad luck all the time. I think that the best thing is to assume that the universe is basically a benign place with enough goodies to go around—the basic glass-half-full view. Then conduct your life with care and diligence, making a modest effort to fill your glass a bit more than half full.

And if the glass breaks and you find your bare butt is on hot sand and your lap is full of lemons, don't despair: it's just bad luck. Buck up, crawl toward a distant cloud, and hope it will soon be raining clean water, sugar, pitchers, glasses, spoons, and cookies.

56. Preparing for the End

As a carbon-based life form, you owe the universe a death. Death is like a whopping balloon payment on a mortgage with a variable term: you're not sure when it's due, you can't refinance, and if you're contemplating early prepayment, you need antidepressants. All you can do about death is make some sensible preparations so the universe doesn't have to track you down and drag you into that sweet, good night kicking and screaming, "Wait, wait! The check's in the mail!"

When my grandmother died during a visit to me and my new wife, it was a mess. Her affairs, as they say, were not in order. Her affairs were in sixteen different shoeboxes in a locked storage space in Winnemucca, Nevada. Soon afterward, although money was tight, we shelled out for our own prepaid cremation with the Neptune Society, so that when we died nobody would have to spring for a traditional funeral. Later, when we had a son and some money that might survive us, we wrote wills. Eventually we set up a trust and made sure our important papers were in a fireproof safe. The safe also has advance directives about how and when to pull the plug, in case we end up as rutabagas on life support in St. Mary's Memorial Storage Locker.

It's a rare dead person who can direct his or her own funeral from beyond the grave, but my Aunt Goldie pulled it off—at least according to her sister, Aunt May. May was a spiritualist who held a séance in her garage every night for a week after her sister died, taking dictation about the color of the casket, the music to play, whether cousin Alfonse would be allowed to attend the wake, and how many beers he could have.

It was weird, sweet, and maddening because Goldie was much more indecisive in death than in life: her spirit kept changing its mind. May's husband, Uncle Salvatore, was up late the night before the burial, glazing the handles on Goldie's casket a darker shade of gold, from Sunset Glow to Bronzy Farewell.

The experience made Uncle Sal overly concerned with preparing for his own end. He prepaid for a fancy funeral, had an advance medical directive so he wouldn't get stuck in a coma, gave a durable power of attorney to his wife and kids, set up revocable and generation-skipping trusts to divvy up his money with scrupulous fairness, and put his birth certificate, stock certificates, bank, and 401(k) account numbers in a safe-deposit box and told everybody where the key was.

The problem was that he wouldn't stop talking about it. Every conversation he had with every relative for a year started out, "When I'm gone ..." He drove everybody so crazy that Aunt May and my cousins exercised their power of attorney a tad early and had him committed to the storage locker.

57. Living in the Senior Moment

I was at a party, talking about old movies, and I had a really perceptive point to make about the star of *The Maltese Falcon*. The trouble was, I couldn't recall who played Sam Spade, so I had to shut up. On the drive home, I turned into my street, ran over my neighbor's garbage can, and realized that I had forgotten trash day again. The next morning my dental hygienist called and asked, "Where are you? We had an appointment at nine."

So there I was, sitting in my kitchen, staring at the coffee grounds and eggshells overflowing out of the garbage can. I was sucking my fuzzy teeth, feeling totally demoralized, when suddenly "Humphrey Bogart" flashed into my mind—twelve hours too late. Thanks a lot, Bogey.

The occasional senior moment is merely irritating. Three in a row is a horrifying taste of what it might be like to live entirely in the senior moment. Increasing memory lapses are inevitable, since the longer you live, the more experience you have to remember with an older brain. For instance, there have been three generations of leading men since Bogart to keep track of. I figure that if I'm forgetting names already, soon I'll forget faces, then to pull up my zipper, then to pull it down.

Thankfully, there are tricks to managing, if not retarding, the slow decline of memory. Here are some I've come up with:

TALK AROUND YOUR MEMORY GAPS

If you stop talking every time you can't remember a name or a term, you'll never get the wrong word in edgewise, much less the right one. So keep talking all around the word you can't remember, describing and defining it until it comes to you, or someone else supplies it: "What would what's-his-name do? You know, that Jewish guy who started Christianity. He was born around 0 BC, died for our sins and all? Oh yeah, that's right: Jesus."

FLIMFLAM WITH VAGUE GENERALITIES

Avoid specifics altogether and talk like a cheap philosopher. Let's say you want to tell your wife, Mary, that you'd like veal parmesan for your seventieth birthday dinner, but you can't recall specifics like her name or the name of the dish or how old you are. Just say, "Meat cooked with cheese is tasty on special occasions." At least it's a complete sentence.

CHANGE THE SUBJECT WITH BODY LANGUAGE

This is my favorite. When my wife and I are chatting and I can't remember a word, I save myself embarrassment by giving her a little hug or squeezing her hand. She appreciates these small expressions of affection so much that she often forgets what we were talking about or the fact that I never answered her last question. Warning: this does not work with authority figures such as traffic cops.

58. Stuff

Stuff moves slowly through my life in a geological process I call "plate tectonics." I started out in life with old plates swiped from my parents, then we got fancy plates as wedding gifts. These gradually broke and were replaced with plastic plates while we raised a family. Then we upgraded to successive generations of nicer and nicer china plates, some bought, some gifted, some collected on travels, some inherited from dead relatives, until we now have enough mismatched plates to serve 142 guests simultaneously, but so little energy that we'd rather just eat a Pop-Tart off a folded paper towel.

Contemplating a move and the horror of packing up all our dishes, we tried to reverse plate tectonics. We gave plates to our son, snuck out of potlucks leaving plates behind, broke plates "accidentally," donated the counterfeit Fiesta Ware to the church jumble sale, and begin thinking about our legacy and who should inherit Aunt Agatha's Spode service for 6.3.

If it were only plates, we might have coped. But it's also furniture and computers and cars and photos and … everything. I pity anyone who has to sort through my stuff after I die.

I finally had to ask for help. I called up my cousin Tati, who is a semiretired life coach. She agreed that stuff accumulates on a geological scale, like sediment deposited at the mouth of the Mississippi.

"You can't have enough kids and grandkids to dredge it all away," she explained. "You need proactive divestiture on the scale of the Army Corps of Engineers. I suggest the Refugee Open House Exercise:

1. "Imagine that the river is rising, and you have to evacuate in ten minutes. Run through your house and grab the Three Ps: pets, pictures, and papers. Maybe a small heirloom like your grandmother's wedding ring. Put these things in the trunk of your car.

2. "Pretend that a Nazi real-estate lady is helping you 'stage' your home for an open house tomorrow. She wants the place almost empty, all surfaces cleared, walls blank, all the funkier furnishings and personal knickknacks gone. Go through each room with a pack of Post-its and stick one on at least two thirds of your furnishings and decorations. Call Goodwill and ask them to come right away for a large pickup. Before they get there, you may rescue enough personal knickknacks to fill the backseat of your car.

3. "When the Goodwill people arrive, ask them to remove all the Post-it-ed items and to lock the house behind them when they leave. Let the dog out of the trunk, put her in the backseat, and drive to Denny's for a chocolate milkshake and a good cry."

I haven't tried the exercise yet, but I was impressed by cousin Tati's expertise. I'm thinking of making her the executor of my estate.

59. Existential Thursday

When you retire, you may experience a spiritual crisis. I generally have mine on Thursdays. On Thursday morning, my blood sugar has crashed from the high of the Wednesday night Dessert Club. I've seen all the movies I want to see at the local multiplex, and the new movies don't open until Friday. My son works, and my wife volunteers on Thursdays, so I'm on my own. Sometimes I'm nostalgic about my ex-colleagues at my old job, thinking of them yukking it up at the Thursday staff meeting.

On Existential Thursdays, gardens need weeding, roofs need shingles, joints need ibuprofen, and hurricane victims need FEMA trailers. Days like these, everything seems to be falling apart, wearing out, washing away, succumbing to chaos. On Thursdays, I often brood about chaos theory, which says that cause and effect are impossible to predict in complex systems. A butterfly flaps its wings in China and starts a chain of events that ultimately results in a hurricane in Louisiana. I fantasize about sending the Marines into China on a surgical strike to terminate that butterfly.

But that would only prevent hurricanes. In the long run, we need to totally demolish chaos. Most Thursdays I combat chaos by working on my order theory.

According to my new order theory, every unfortunate event happens for a reason. The universe is not running down. It is evolving into a different, better kind of order that is too cosmic and profound for me to understand. When the universe seems chaotic, it's because my human intelligence is too limited to see the grand design. I can only see the downside of gophers and AIDS and reality TV because I lack imagination and the cosmic point of view. Somehow, all the things that bug me are connected in a murky but benevolent plan.

To make sense of the apparent chaos of the universe, I postulate the existence of a superior intelligence behind the surface appearance of things, running the show like the Wizard of Oz behind the screen. That makes me feel better. It's still Existential Thursday, but I'm in the Emerald City. I've got my green glasses on, and nobody can tell me that pumpkins are orange and water is clear. I know better.

Thankfully, the next day is Good Friday, when I come to my senses and realize that I have wandered off into theology and counting my blessings. And anyway, it doesn't matter, because there are new movies opening tonight.

60. Your Life List

One morning I was making my usual retirement breakfast: four Weight-Watchers-points' worth of oatmeal and my daily eight-ounce allotment of real coffee. It seemed like my life had become like my diet—sensible, dull, and too soon gone. Just as I was asking myself, "Is that all there is?" a guy on the radio started talking about making a Life List.

Although the Internet is the primary information conduit of the twenty-first century, God speaks to me most often through the radio, in the voices of anonymous interviewees who all sound like Deepak Chopra. This time he was telling me to make a Life List of all my long-cherished goals and set about achieving them before he pulled my plug.

I had heard about this Life List deal before, from my Uncle Horace. When he retired from selling tires at Wheel World, he created a Life List to help him achieve his lifelong ambition, becoming an international jewel thief like Cary Grant in *To Catch a Thief.* He started small, dressing up in a tuxedo to shoplift Cracker Jacks for the plastic diamond-ring prizes. Right under the noses of the checkers at the all-night grocery store, he broke into one of those oversized gumball machines and made off with all the capsules containing rhinestone bracelets. In New Orleans, he stole Mardi Gras beads from the gutter. He taught himself lock picking so he could burglarize pawnshops for defective engagement rings. His biggest score was swiping Madonna's tongue stud from the Rock and Roll Hall of Fame.

Uncle Horace was finally caught outside Manny's Credit Jewelers and Cell Phone Emporium with a Burger King bag full of cubic zirconias. But even this was part of his fiendishly clever master plan. He feigned dementia and was committed to a facility for the criminally insane, where he was taken care of for the rest of his life in conditions superior to those at the average retirement community, straitjackets and group therapy notwithstanding.

The radio guy said to include some smaller, more quickly achievable goals on your Life List. This made me think of my Uncle Elmo, who simply wanted to balance his checkbook to the penny before he died. He finally did it at age seventy-eight, when he hadn't written any checks for several months. My Aunt Ida always wanted to get back at the raccoons that knocked over her garbage can at night. Her Life List helped her figure out that by keeping all the garbage under her bed, the can would be empty and would stop attracting raccoons.

I decided to start small with my Life List, so I set the goal of having a second cup of real coffee. That was easily accomplished and filled me with enough energy to make some slightly more ambitious additions to the list, such as cleaning out the hall closet, losing ten pounds, and walking on the moon.

61. Writing Your Own Epitaph

The raccoons killed another chicken last week, and I had to bury it out by the septic tank. It got me thinking about writing my own epitaph, which is a classic encounter-group exercise from the sixties. It's designed to clarify values, spur insight, and bum out a whole roomful of people at once.

Writing your own epitaph can sum up your life so far, highlight what's really important to you, send a message to the future, express your philosophy of life, and get in a final dig at your family. Epitaphs can range from the sublime ("I'D RATHER BE IN PHILADELPHIA" —W. C. Fields) to the ridiculous ("POET, HERO, STATESMAN" —I. M. A. Putz).

Some people have taken this exercise so seriously that they actually write their epitaph into their wills. If you actually intend to have your composition carved into stone, be brief. Stone carving is expensive, and graveyard visitors are poor readers. Their eyes are often full of tears, and they have short attention spans because they want to get out of the weather and back to the reception where they can have a drink.

When I visit an old graveyard, I always appreciate the rare inscription that mentions the cause of death: "1918, SPANISH FLU" or "CALLED HOME BY ANGELS." I wish more people would follow this charming custom with updated versions for our times: "HAIR DRYER IN TUB," "INFARCTION," or "ASLEEP AT THE WHEEL." Come to think of it, you can't write one of these ahead of time—unless you're contemplating suicide, in which case, see the chapters on the doldrums and Existential Thursday.

Some cheapskates just put their family name on a single stone, with no first names or dates, so they can use the stone for several generations. For myself, I'd rather be distinguished as an individual. Sharing a stone is too much like sharing a toothbrush.

For the marker itself, stone will soon be passé. Any favorite object of the deceased can now be laser scanned, blown up larger than life on a 3-D printer, and cast into plastic resin. Cemeteries will soon be much more interesting to browse because of the giant plastic violins, cell phones, wrenches, body parts, and so on.

The more I think about it, the more I am inclined to go ahead and design my own dream funeral. This is actually something of a tradition in my family. My Aunt Raynal plans to be frozen solid and pounded into Morro Bay by a pile driver. Cousin Biff will be buried in his '56 Rambler Metro convertible. But not all of us are that flamboyant. Uncle Filmore, a kitchen contractor, had a perfectly conventional funeral, but his tombstone was made out of Corian. I'm planning to have a green funeral myself: no embalming, a plain wood casket, a papier-mâché tombstone, and manicured nails, all painted green.

62. Mental-Illness Day

According to the experts, you can retire and stay young, active, and healthy by eating mostly fruits and vegetables, exercising for two hours every day, drinking lots of water, flossing your teeth, doing crossword puzzles to keep your mind sharp, surrounding yourself with loved ones, keeping a full calendar of social events and obligations, having pets, traveling, meditating, taking classes, volunteering, and so on and on and on. You won't live forever, but it will seem like it.

Remember when you were working and you got so stressed out you had to take a mental-health day? You can't do that anymore because you're retired now and in your golden years, when everything is hunky-dory. So retired people need to take occasional mental-illness days—days when they don't eat right, don't socialize, don't take their little walks or pottery classes, don't live the careful, reasonable, safe lives they've been advised to live.

On your mental-illness day, you can stay in bed till noon. You can have cold pizza for breakfast. You can remove the skin from the chicken breast, throw the meat away, and eat the skin. You can pick things up using your lower back muscles instead of your legs. You can not wear your seat belt and fail to come to a full, complete stop at stop signs. You can ignore the doorbell and hang up on people you don't want to talk to on the phone. You can sit too close to the TV and run with scissors—or at least walk fast with them.

I like to save my favorite bad habits for Mental-Illness Day. I read trashy novels, watch the shopping channel, slouch on the couch, put my feet up on the coffee table, eat the whole pint of Chubby Hubby, discard my absentee ballot, skip meetings, and rant about the government.

On a mental-illness day, you can indulge in your guiltiest pleasures and most annoying personality traits. You can forget to take your meds, overdraw your account, turn your hearing aid off, miss deadlines, skip the shower, pick at scabs, wear yesterday's clothes, park in the red zone, screen your calls, and tell people the truth or lies—whatever's easier or most fun.

I think of Mental-Illness Day as a vacation from responsibility, a way of relieving the pressure of my golden years before I blow up entirely. Retired people are supposed to be a regimented flock of sheep, all trudging patiently in neat parallel lines toward the final cliff of death. Just for one day, don't be a sheep! Be a wild-assed lemming and make a mad dash for the finish line!

If your mental-illness day leaves you tired, guilty, headachy, and sick to your stomach, you can always get back into line tomorrow.

63. Inside Out

If you're of retirement age, you know that bad experiences in the past can affect your present mood, and that people tend to make the same mistakes over and over. But that's not complicated enough for psychologists. They could tell us that on the phone, without having us come in once a week for years at ninety bucks a pop. So, to provide some job security, they have invented theories, models, modalities, protocols, and so on—elaborate metaphors that boil down to "history repeats itself."

One of my favorite psychometaphorical friends is John Bradshaw's "inner child." According to John, inside every person there is a newborn, an infant, a toddler, a school kid, an adolescent, and so on—all the way up to an inner version of who you were just yesterday. It's like those Russian nesting dolls, one inside another inside another.

If one of those inner versions of you had a particularly hard time, it goes missing. It fades from consciousness and disappears. This is like when the littlest Russian doll rolls under the radiator and you have a vague feeling of emptiness for twenty years. This feeling lasts until you finally rip out the boiler and install a forced-air furnace and remove the radiators and "Oh! Look what I found!"

The goal of inner-child work is to bring all the troubled inner selves into the light, give them their say, and reassemble the Russian doll into a coherent, contemporaneous personality that is resilient, positive, and skilled in meeting the challenges of everyday life. But of course, nobody ever does that. We are all damaged goods to some extent, our inner selves huddled on the dark sidewalk of our superego while our id goes up in flames, held together with moral barbed wire and the yellow crime-scene tape of guilt, crying because our psychic credit cards got burnt up and we have no safe place to sleep tonight.

But hey, we're used to that. Even if your inner child is a milk-carton kid, by the time you retire you have enough inner selves to play a humongous game of capture the flag, although your youngest selves are too little to play and your older selves have pulled groins and can't recall what side they're on.

When I tire of the drab outer layer of retirement, I turn myself inside out and let one of the younger, more colorful selves play for a while. I let the rebellious teen go for a motorcycle ride. I let the precocious third-grader draw a picture. I let the hungry infant have some warm milk and go to sleep.

Good night.

Patrick Fanning is a retired publisher, painter, and author who talked himself into writing just one more book, but after this he is definitely going to retire for good, whether he can afford it or not. He has authored and coauthored many books, including *Messages*, *Self Esteem*, and *Thoughts & Feelings*. He started a second career painting landscapes about twelve years ago, but he's more or less retired from that as well. He is contemplating a third career as a filmmaker, comedian, singer/songwriter, handyman, or human drug trial subject—he hasn't decided yet.

Patrick's retirement activities include woodworking, messing with pianos and harpsichords, flying, listening to music, painting, restoring old cars, cooking, fixing up old houses, volunteering at the art center and film society, riding his recumbent bike, and having coffee with friends. He says, "I like to think of myself as a Renaissance man—if the Renaissance happened in twenty-first century Sonoma County among a passel of disillusioned hippies, red diaper yuppies, and failed dot-commers—kind of Renaissance Lite."

He lives in rural northern California with his wife Nancy, a calico cat, six chickens, many gophers, rats, mice, and birds, and a septic tank full of assorted micro-organisms. If he has paid his ISP bill and hasn't screwed things up again, his website can be found at www.fanningartworks.com.

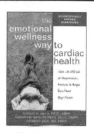

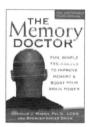
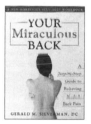